angelfish

braz walker

t.f.h.

PHOTOGRAPHY

Dr. Herbert R. Axelrod: 27 (bottom), 45, 48, 49, 50, 53, 56, 61, 65, 66, 69, 72, 81; Wolfgang Bechtle: 36; Franz Driessens: 21 (top); James Dunbar: 128; Stanislav Frank: 33 (bottom); Robert Gannon: 29 (top), 110 (top); Dr. Rolf Geisler: 28 (left); General Biological Supply House: 24 (top); H.A. Gitlin: 83; H. Helmert: 24 (bottom), 121; Paul Imgrund: 29 (bottom); Dr. W.T. Innes: 40; Ray Juschkus: 68; J. Knaack: 28 (right); M. Kocar: 43; Lakeview Fish Hatcheries: 73; Franz Lazi: 41; K. Lerch: 27 (top); Horst Mueller: 8; Klaus Paysan: 1, 4, 31, 44, 87, 103, 107, 125; Helmut Pinter: 37, 93, 98; H.J. Richter: 64, 77 (bottom), 84, 85, 88, 89; Harald Schultz: 38; Dr. Duncan Sculthorpe: 19, 21 (bottom); Tierfreunde: 52, 76, 80; G.J.M. Timmerman: 59, 115; Gene Wolfsheimer: 57; Peter Wong: 77 (top), 92; Ruda Zukal: 33 (top), 96, 100, 101, 123

ISBN 0-87666-022-7

Distributed in the U.S.A. by T.F.H. Publications, Inc., 211 West Sylvania Avenue, P.O. Box 27, Neptune City, N.J. 07753; in England by T.F.H. (Gt. Britain) Ltd., 13 Nutley Lane, Reigate, Surrey; in Canada by Clarke, Irwin & Company, Clarwin House, 791 St. Clair Avenue West, Toronto 10, Ontario; in Southeast Asia by Y. W. Ong, 9 Lorong 36 Geylang, Singapore 14; in Australia and the south Pacific by Pet Imports Pty. Ltd., P.O. Box 149, Brookvale 2100, N.S.W., Australia.
Published by T.F.H. Publications, Inc. Ltd., The British Crown Colony of Hong Kong.

CONTENTS

Graceful, intelligent, hardy, easy to feed, with interesting breeding habits. . . the angelfish embodies many of the most important good points of the ideal aquarium inhabitant.

INTRODUCTION

Angelfish have been called "kings of the aquarium," and not without justification. Other fishes come and go, and a few even become established favorites in the aquarium hobby, but since the introduction of angelfish about 1911 they have held a unique position in the fishkeeping world. There is about them a regal grace, a dignity, a presence, which could hardly be associated with less than royalty, and in an aquarium angelfish are so immediately striking that even those completely unfamiliar with fishes and uninterested in them will single them out and ask about them. Over the years angelfish have caught the eye and imagination of countless non-aquarists and turned them into aquarists.

Scientifically, there are three generally recognized angelfish species which have been kept in the aquarium, and one other which has not. Further study may prove one or more of these fishes to be synonymous, or to belong to the same species. *Pterophyllum scalare* was the first to be kept by aquarists, followed by *Pterophyllum eimekei*, and in recent years a few wild specimens of *Pterophyllum altum* have been imported. *Pterophyllum dumerilii* apparently has not been imported.

Angelfish (and here I am of course talking specifically about the fishes of the genus *Pterophyllum*, not about the marine angelfish, which are in a different family entirely) belong to the family Cichlidae, a large family of perch-like fishes found mostly in South and Central America and in Africa. In appearance, however, angelfish are among the least perchlike of cichlids, for their bodies are thin and laterally flattened or compressed; the dorsal and anal fins are very long and almost wing-like, the ventral fins have developed into long "feelers," and the pointed front end of the fish terminates in a mouth that is proportionately much smaller than that of most other cichlids. The sides of the fish in all wild *Pterophyllum* species are adorned with several handsome vertical black stripes that contrast strikingly with the lighter spaces between. These light spaces range in color from yellowish to bluish silver, varying with the species.

Because of their stateliness and great beauty, angelfish commanded high prices for years after their introduction. Dr. William T. Innes recalled that they sold for $75 a pair when first seen in the United States after having been imported to Hamburg, Germany in 1911, and Dr. George S. Myers found them selling for that price in Philadelphia in 1917. When you consider the much greater value of $75 then as contrasted to now and consider also that the two fish offered as a "pair" might turn out not to be a pair at all, you have a good appreciation of the relative expensiveness of angelfish at that time. Those who purchased angelfish at such prices often did so as an investment. Aquarists of that time (circa 1920) had to know how to "fly by the seat of their pants" or operate by feel much better than the aquarist of today with his multitude of equipment and accessories. There was little literature available, and there were very few power filters, pH kits, brine shrimp eggs, sub-sand filters, all-glass tanks, air pumps, automatic heaters, packaged remedies, frozen, freeze-dried and scientifically formulated flake foods which we take for granted today; some of these items were absent entirely. Early breeders relied almost completely on experience-acquired skill to maintain and reproduce their fishes. Considering the difficulties which even modern equipment-rich aquarium hobbyists often encounter, they were fantastically successful. Lacking all but the most primitive aeration, filtration and heating devices and using

Aquarium hobbyists of today have available to them many more different items of equipment, accessories and foodstuffs than could be obtained by aquarists operating at the time the angelfish was first introduced into the hobby. Brine shrimp eggs, frozen and freeze-dried foods, reliable thermostatic heaters, power filters and many other products taken for granted by modern hobbyists were out of the reach of old-time fish fanciers. Considering the handicaps under which they worked, the old-timers did very well.

Although it is a cichlid and therefore shares with its cousins within the family certain basic characters that differentiate fishes of the family Cichlidae from other species, the angelfish is different in shape from the most commonly seen cichlid species, being much more noticeably laterally compressed and having an over-all much more delicate appearance than any of the chunky or torpedo-shaped cichlids.

iron-framed aquariums which periodically rusted and required repainting, they regularly collected natural foods for their fishes and often formulated their own prepared foods. Success, especially in breeding, was often preceded by many failures, but they persevered through their love of what they were doing, and their efforts formed the early links of the great chain of knowledge which is available to us today. Wild-caught angelfish were . . . and still are . . . among the most difficult of fishes to breed. Even now (late 1973) no one has spawned *Pterophyllum altum* even though many breeders are trying.

GENERAL REQUIREMENTS

Angelfish are excellent aquarium occupants and show great adaptability to a wide variety of environmental conditions. With good care they can live for many years in the aquarium and, while their requirements are not elaborate, there are certain needs and limitations which the aquarist should be aware of to keep them at their best. While the requirements for successful breeding are a bit more stringent than those concerning simply their keeping, these will be discussed under "BREEDING." The following are more basic considerations to assure their well-being.

The Aquarium

Whether angelfish are kept in an aquarium by themselves or with other fishes in a "community" situation, it should be remembered that they are cichlids capable of growing to a large size and should therefore be given plenty of room. Actually, the larger the aquarium, the better, and crowding should be avoided.

Only a few years ago one of the major considerations in the selection of an aquarium for any purpose was to pick one which had as much air surface as possible in relation to its capacity. Modern equipment, such as reliable air pumps and filters, gives us more latitude for the selection of various shapes of aquariums without sacrificing the advantages provided by increased capacity. More aquariums are seen today which are tall and thin, with relatively little air surface for their volume. With tall and graceful fish such as angels, a very pleasing scene can be created by utilizing some of the taller and thinner designs with

Tall tanks have an obvious advantage over low tanks in the housing of angelfish in that they provide the greater depth that allows the planting of tall plants, and they are more esthetically in line with the shape of the fish. Long, low tanks can be used, however, and are very useful for housing young angels in quantity; they provide more surface area per unit of volume and are easier to maintain.

their more "square-faced" approach in contrast to the conventional rectangular look. If you should prefer the taller and thinner design, it should be kept in mind that the aquarium should be well aerated and that if the air pump should stop for one reason or another the fish in such an aquarium with its limited air surface/water ratio will show signs of breathing distress sooner than in longer and lower models. It is even more important for this reason to avoid overcrowding, and a small, inexpensive air pump kept in reserve as a "spare tire" is worthwhile insurance.

Modern aquariums, with the exception of custom sizes which sometimes employ angle iron or angle aluminum, are generally of two kinds. The conventional stainless steel framed aquarium is still quite popular, and still considered by some manufacturers to be their "deluxe" line. Over the last few years, however, there has been a tremendous increase in the popularity of "all-glass" aquariums.

Stainless steel aquariums employ a stainless steel frame which is usually spot-welded where the pieces join. The bottom is usually glass or slate, and it and the glasses are held in place by a tar-base aquarium cement applied in a hot and plastic state when the aquarium is assembled. Individual glasses which become broken are not difficult to remove and replace, and some of these aquariums have been in service for many years. Occasionally one will start to leak a bit, and this can usually be fixed by cleaning and thoroughly drying, after which liquid aquarium cement or Asphaltum B varnish can be run down the seams and allowed to dry, sealing the leak, or a seam of silicone rubber aquarium cement can be applied to the inner seams of the clean and dry aquarium. Either of these should be allowed to dry for 48 hours. Use *only* silicone rubber which is packaged for aquarium use, since other types may contain fungicides or other harmful substances that could be detrimental to your fish.

All-glass aquariums are constructed of pre-cut, pre-fitted glass for the bottom as well as the sides, and each piece of glass is simply cemented to the others with silicone rubber. This compound has such great strength that no other bonding or support is necessary, provided that the compound is properly applied and that the glass is of great enough strength to stand the weight of the water to be contained. Some manufacturers employ a plastic or other frame similar to molding which fits around the top of the aquarium and the bottom. The corners are still free of visual obstruction, and these frames facilitate assembly as well as often enhancing the appearance of the aquarium. Glass aquariums have the added advantage of often being somewhat less expensive than conventional stainless steel aquariums.

Temperature

The temperature of even equatorial jungle streams and rivers fluctuates more than one might imagine, and for this reason angelfish have a considerable range of temperatures which to them are tolerable. While the extremes at either the high or low end should be avoided if possible, especially for extended periods of time, they can be tolerated for brief periods without apparent detriment to the fish. This is especially true in a large aquarium and if wide fluctuations do not occur within too brief a period of time.

Generally, the temperature limits should be considered to be within a range of 65 to 85°F. although 5 degrees can be extended at the upper and lower limits if the time is brief and the aquarium is well aerated and filtered. For ordinary maintenance of angelfish, a temperature of around 75°F. could be considered ideal. At this temperature they are quite active, and growth is excellent. Breeding can be stimulated in mature fish by a rise in temperature to 80–82°F. combined with a partial water change.

European aquarists are less inclined than Americans to try to maintain a steady temperature, allowing the temperature to fall a few degrees at night and rise again the next day. The theory is that this is a healthful practice, since it is what occurs in nature.

Maintaining a desirable temperature for tropicals is no longer a problem. A number of reputable and dependable manufacturers produce excellent automatic heaters in a wide variety of styles and wattages. While separate thermostats and heaters are still in use, much more popular are the integrated single-tube units which contain both

Hanging thermometer.

Floating thermometer.

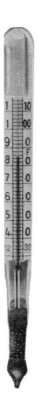

A good thermometer is a wise investment for any aquarist; in high tanks it sometimes is a good idea to have more than one thermometer, one situated at the bottom and one at the top, so that wide variations between temperature at different levels of the tank can be easily detected.

thermostat and heater as well as a capacitor (condenser) to eliminate radio and television interference. There are also two-tube integrated units which house heater and thermostat separately for the theoretical purpose of not having heat produced within the tube by the heater affect the ability of the thermostat to read the water temperature. In practice, the two systems seem to work out equally well, and most aquarists will find the single-tube models much more convenient. Settings are made by a knob on top of the part of the heater housing which hangs on the side of the aquarium above the water.

The wattage of the heater to be used depends mostly on the size of the aquarium. There is an old (but workable) rule of thumb allowing 5 watts per gallon. Because of water's great capacity to store heat, this figure is somewhat adjustable on a sliding scale downward as the size of the aquarium increases, and except for occasions of great differential between ambient and desired temperatures, a 200-watt heater is probably adequate for a 100-gallon aquarium. This is the largest size heater ordinarily manu-factured in an automatic unit. If more wattage is required, the separate thermostat and heater system can be used, since thermostats can be purchased with capacities up to 500 or 600 watts, and heaters can be added by plugging into the thermostat unit until the desired wattage is reached. Of course several heaters may be used in the same tank.

While there are economy lines of heaters available which are quite good value, more expensive models are generally more accurate, more dependable and less likely to cause radio and television interference. Cheap heaters sometimes fail and have been known to "cook" a tankful of fish. It is better to spend a bit more and be confident of a reliable unit with prized fishes. In general, it is best to buy only' equipment which is nationally advertised in hobbyist magazines and recommended by your aquarium dealer.

Lighting

Lighting an aquarium, whether for display purposes or for a breeding aquarium, can have a number of effects not only on the appearance of the fish involved and their surroundings, but also on the physical conditions within the tank and the manner in which the inhabitants react to them. Light serves both to allow the aquarist to view the underwater scene and to promote the growth of plants if they are present, since proper illumination is necessary for the process of photosynthesis, a vital function for living plants.

It is difficult to beat Nature at her own work and for growing most plants nothing is quite the equal of natural sunlight. While natural daylight can make plants thrive if, for instance, an aquarium is situated in front of a window, other problems can arise through the use of daylight for illumination. The intensity of daylight changes from season to season, and in midsummer the brightness of the illumination may cause an insurmountable algae problem, whereas in winter there may be too little light for plant growth. This, of course, can be compensated for, but the backlighting of an aquarium from outside gives a less pleasing effect even when supplemented by an aquarium light than if the backlighting were excluded.   Direct sun often overheats an aquarium . . . beware!

Aquariums equipped with artificially lighted hoods answer the questions of providing controllable illumination, and in the case of Gro-lux (Sylvania) or Plant-gro (Westinghouse) fluorescent tubes the light provided is of comparable quality to daylight as far as plant growth is concerned. The light thus provided also enhances the colors of many fishes, being rich in both the red and blue ends of the spectrum in comparison to other lighting, and also has the added advantage of coolness and low power consumption offered by fluorescent lighting. If a full-cover hood is used, evaporation is retarded and fish can't

All-glass tank equipped with reflector and glass cover to provide full-hood coverage.

The big advantage of the full-hood reflector over the strip reflector is that it gives much greater protection against loss of fish through jumping while also conserving heat and reducing evaporation. Additionally, it keeps the tank cleaner and reduces chances of having harmful substances dropped into the tank. The disadvantages are that full hoods cost much more than strip reflectors and make the tank too warm during protracted hot spells.

jump out. If a "strip" or half-cover light is used, supplementary stainless steel strips can be obtained to cover the rear half. Plastic and aluminum supplementary covers are also available, or a strip of glass can serve the purpose. Provision is made on most of these supplementary units and on the full-cover hoods for holes to be punched out or cut out for installation of heaters, filters, etc. While angelfish are perhaps not the most notorious jumpers among aquarium fishes, don't delude yourself into thinking they won't take an occasional aerial excursion. As with the usual trend of such things, the dried, mummified corpse on the floor next morning is invariably the best fish in the bunch. It seems like runts don't jump.

Hoods also come equipped with incandescent lights. Incandescent hoods and bulbs are initially less expensive, but more power is consumed for a given amount of lighting and bulbs burn out much more often. Incandescent lights also generate considerable heat.

One prime advantage in the use of regular aquarium reflectors of any type is that lighting is provided from above, which not only is the most enhancing angle for most fishes, but also is from a constantly predictable direction to which the fish become quickly accustomed. Because of this, even fish like angels, once notorious for "heart attacks," are less likely to suffer severe fright from being suddenly flooded with illumination from an unexpected source. This was especially problematical some years ago when fish had arrived after a long, often cold journey in shipping cans, the dead inner blackness of which might be suddenly flooded with brightness on arrival. While turning on the aquarium lights is certainly less traumatic and angels are much less prone to shock than they once were, it is still wise to give a couple of "warning taps" on the aquarium before suddenly turning on the light, especially in a darkened room.

Rolf Kübler wrote a very instructive paperback book, *"Light in the Aquarium,"* which covers most things you need to know about the subject. Get hold of a copy and study it. With a solid understanding of light and its aquarium considerations, you can have more success as an aquarist.

Live Plants for Angels

Observation can often give useful clues to aspects of the natural environment of a creature. Long, slender legs on an animal can indicate swiftness, while shorter more heavily structured limbs and bodies may be more indicative of strength and great stamina. While such physical attributes can give an idea of some aspects of an animal's lifestyle, coloration and pattern can be equally informative at times concerning the surrounding environmental conditions toward which a creature has evolved in nature. The prominent vertical striping of angelfishes is a good example.

As the alternating black bars and white areas would seem to indicate, angels live mostly among upreaching and downhanging plant structures, naturally camouflaged to an extent by their shading, which blends them in with the hanging roots of floating plants and the rising leaves and stems of bottom-rooted ones. The fact that nature would trouble to endow them with the ability to blend out of sight so well would seem to suggest the idea that under similar conditions they might be more at ease and responsive to the efforts of the aquarist. For those who wish to provide a "natural" setting for their angels there are a

Map of northern South America showing recorded distribution of the recognized angelfish species. From *Review of South American Freshwater Angelfishes—Genus Pterophyllum*, by Dr. Leonard P. Schultz. Volume 120, Number 3555 (1967) of the Proceedings of the United States National Museum.

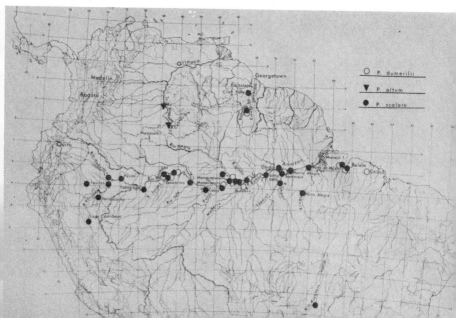

Echinodorus species, one of the favored plants used by angelfish keepers for both decorative value and utility as spawning medium.

number of excellent and readily available domestic aquarium plants from which to choose. Angelfish fortunately do not have the inherent urge to uproot and otherwise destroy plants as well as digging holes in the aquarium substrate like so many of their cichlid relatives.

Perhaps the classic aquarium plant to be associated with angelfish is the Amazon swordplant. Actually, several similar species of the genus *Echinodorus* are known collectively as "Amazon swords" and are distinguished by such popular names as "wide leaf swordplant," "narrow leaf swordplant," etc. Their tall and graceful leaves make these among the most handsome and desirable of so-called "center plants," and the width and strength of the leaves make them excellent receivers for the spawn of angels. As a matter of fact, they seem actually to be the preferred medium most often in cases where the fish have a wide range of choices.

Giant *Sagittaria* is also a choice plant for receiving the eggs of angelfish as well as for furnishing their tank in a natural manner. This is also a broad-leaved and impressive "center plant," . . . which does not necessarily mean that the plant should be placed in the middle of the aquarium, but only that it is large enough that it may be used as a focal point or center of attention. The species referred to here as "giant" has leaves which reach a width comparable to the swordplants, perhaps $1\frac{1}{2}''$.

The larger species of *Cryptocoryne* are also among the chosen spawn receivers for angelfish. *Cryptocoryne* species are especially useful in low-light situations, since they require less illumination than most other aquatic plants. There are several species available of such diverse forms and dimensions that an aquarium can be very attractively decorated using only *Cryptocoryne* species. They grow rather slowly, but the leaves of larger crypts upon which angels are likely to spawn are quite tough and sturdy, enabling them to well endure the rigors of cleaning imposed upon them by prospective parent angels.

For "background plants" it is difficult to find better ones which are either more beautiful or easier to grow than the old standby and favorite, *Vallisneria spiralis*, either in its original form or in its so-called "corkscrew" form. For larger and deeper tanks there are longer and broader-leaved species available, and the slender, graceful leaves of the various *Vallisneria* species accentuate the form and markings of angelfish.

Sagittaria species are quite similar grass-like plants which encompass species that can fill roles similar to those of the *Vallisneria* species. *Sagittaria* species, however,

Cryptocoryne nevillii.

Vallisneria spiralis.

Sagittaria graminea

have tougher and sturdier leaves and are a bit less graceful, since they, unlike *Vallisneria*, do not "sway" with the motions of the fish.

Other plants which grow well in the aquarium and please the taste of the aquarist are certainly useful also. For the specialized care of angelfish, however, it is recommended that you select types which are not difficult to keep. It is probably best to keep the number of species down also, picking perhaps two or even three which can fill the required roles but which won't need continual pruning, re-setting, etc., all of which can be disturbing to the fish. This is not to indicate that angelfish are meek, frightened and "scary" creatures which will think the sky is falling every time an acorn drops. They are far from such, and at times can be surprisingly bold. At the same time they do not benefit from undue disturbances. As a matter of fact, this is true of any fish.

Feeding Angelfish

Angelfish are predatory by nature, feeding under natural conditions on various bite-size aquatic creatures such as crustaceans, aquatic insects and larvae, small fishes and other living things which happen to come their way. As with most predatory aquarium fishes, their number one choice in the aquarium is living food similar to that which would comprise their fare in nature. Fortunately, however, angelfish are perfectly suited to the wide variety of excellent dry foods which are available for aquarium fishes today.

Well-maintained angels are eager eaters and quickly flock to any recognizable food dropped into their tank; here a group of adult angels are eating live bloodworms.

There are a number of prepared fish foods available which so closely approximate the nourishment qualities of natural foods that the urban apartment dweller who must rely strictly on what he can buy to feed his fish can expect to raise angels of size and quality almost equal to those produced by another aquarist who has access to various live foods which he may collect for himself. Frozen

Adult brine shrimp.

Bloodworm

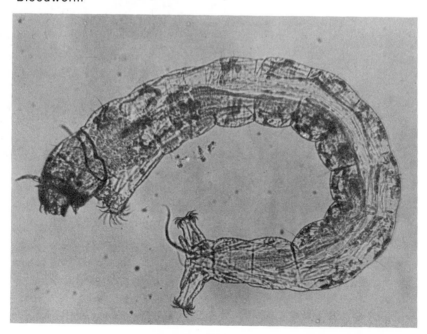

brine shrimp, *Daphnia*, mosquito larvae and others can be purchased, while freeze-dried versions of these "natural" foods are also available, and very little nutritional value is sacrificed in processing. Frozen clams, shrimp, etc., normally sold for marine fishes, are often very suitable for feeding your angels.

Perhaps today's real "staple" fish food, if one type can be nominated above the others, is the amazingly high quality flake fish food upon which so many aquarists rely. There are several brands of flake food, most of which are imported, which are so well balanced that many fishes will thrive on one of them alone, not supplemented by other foods. Such an exclusive feeding program is not advocated, since a bit of variety in the diet tends to generate more zest and enthusiasm in our fishes, especially angels. Without trying to anthropomorphize angelfish, most of us would agree that a nutritionally perfect, laboratory-prepared diet which consisted of only one food item which never changed in texture, taste or appearance would become rather tiresome.

Ground beef heart is an excellent food. For young angels it can be blended, while for older ones twice through the fine blade on a food grinder is adequate. Fat and vein material or connecting tissue should be removed before grinding. Beef heart can be kept frozen in balls which are adequate for one feeding. It can also be "stretched" by blending or fine grinding and adding to plain gelatin which has been prepared according to directions. The beef heart and gelatin should be folded together or gently stirred together while the gelatin is still in a liquid state. Don't try to mix them in a blender or with a mixer, since air bubbles will also be mixed in which won't rise in the thick gelatin, resulting in the final gelled food's floating instead of sinking. After mixing, pour onto a cookie sheet if you wish, and chill. Usable pieces can be easily cut with a dull knife and frozen. By slicing very thin, long strips, and cutting to the desired length, "worms" can be cut which float down in a most interesting and enticing way. The added gelatin is not simply padding, because gelatin is about 85% protein.

Living food, when available, is of course preferred by the fish above all other foods. Angelfish particularly enjoy the chase of living, moving objects, and among their favorites are mosquito larvae, known in some areas as "wiggle-tails," bloodworms, which are the larvae of non-biting midges of the family Tendipedidae, *Daphnia* or "water fleas," white worms or enchytrae, small earthworms and *Tubifex*. Especially relished, but hardly suppliable in quantities to keep several large angels going, are baby guppies and babies of other livebearing species. Without doubt these create the greatest excitement to be seen in an angelfish tank, although many aquarists object to feeding live fish to fish. I personally do not particularly advocate or object to the practice, but it should be remembered that the major food for fishes in nature is other fishes, and even in the guppy tank there are probably many more baby guppies eaten by their parents than ever reach full size. One thing which might be remembered is that should a prized angelfish go "off his feed," baby guppies are as likely as anything to start it feeding once more. This problem seldom occurs in clean, well cared-for aquariums.

For those who enjoy collecting live foods, the best can often be collected from the cleanest places. Both mosquitoes and the little gnats or midges which are responsible for the larvae which we call bloodworms will lay their eggs on almost any calm water surface. The larvae are often found in man-made receptacles (or even unoccupied fish ponds) which happen to have caught a little rain water and where perhaps a few rotten leaves are present for nourishment.

While almost everyone is familiar with the larvae of mosquitoes, some may be less so with the larvae of

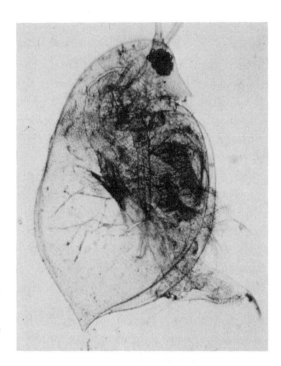

Daphnia

Tubifex worms

tendipedid midges, or bloodworms. These larvae live in the organic "mud" formed by decaying vegetation, in little cylindrical chambers which they construct around themselves. An interesting point is that the reason for the red coloration of these worm-like creatures is due to a red blood pigment called erythrocruorin, the presence of which allows them to live in water that is severely depleted of oxygen.

Earthworms and white worms can of course be raised by the aquarist in a small box of compost kept in a cool place. If room permits, Styrofoam fish shipping containers are excellent worm beds. They can be filled with half garden soil and half leaf mould or peat moss. Bread crusts, oatmeal, cornmeal, etc., serve as food for the worms. More elaborate instructions on their care can be obtained from

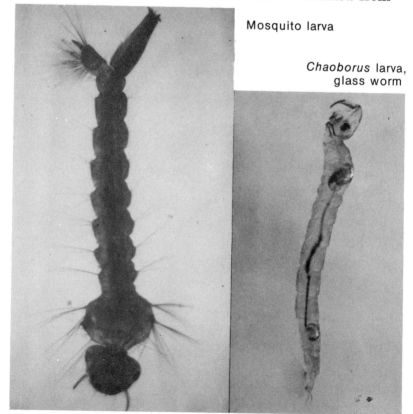

Mosquito larva

Chaoborus larva, glass worm

White worms

Earthworms

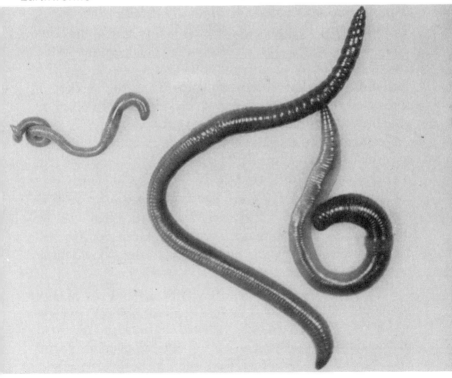

most dealers who handle them or from a number of the larger handbooks on aquarium keeping in general. Several books dealing with the mechanics of raising live foods are available, one of the newest and most comprehensive being *Live Foods for Aquarium and Terrarium Animals*, published by T.F.H. Publications; this book is obtainable at pet shops everywhere.

Daphnia can be collected at various times of the year from most permanently standing, fish-free bodies of water. Better still, since it is safer concerning introduction of parasites or other disease organisms sometimes present in *Daphnia* ponds, get a starter culture and raise your own in a suitable container. Excellent for this purpose are the various sizes of vinyl wading pools which are quite reasonably priced.

Live brine shrimp and tubifex are available at times from larger aquarium shops. Both are excellent fish foods. Tubifex must be properly cleaned before use by flushing away dead worms and debris with cool running water. Because of the unclean conditions under which they live in nature, they have been named as being the carriers of some of the strange diseases which occasionally occur in angelfish and discus, especially discus.

Feeding adult angels twice a day is desirable, although once will do if the other is impossible. For those who can manage, even a third feeding is desirable, in which case feedings can be a bit more sparing so that the food is thoroughly cleaned up. Never feed more than can be consumed by the fish in a few minutes. Healthier fish will be produced by feeding just short of what would have completely satisfied them.

Foods can be alternated for variety, routinely if you wish. An example would be frozen brine shrimp morning and evening with flake food between, or perhaps flake food in the morning and frozen shrimp in the evening if you feed twice a day. Another food such as beef heart might

The best tankmates for angelfish are other angelfish. . . but if you want to mix and match species in a community tank, you don't have much of a problem, because there are many species with which angels will live in harmony. Just avoid the obvious troublemakers like puffers and other fin-nippers as well as the species whose requirements as regards water temperature and condition are very much different from those of angelfish.

substitute for one of these, or perhaps live food regularly once or twice a week. Good nutrition pays off in good fish, and feeding is to most fishkeepers the most enjoyable part of their avocation; it also challenges the aquarist to provide nutrition which will bring his angelfish to their best and keep them there.

Suitable Companions for Angelfish

Angelfish are unfortunately often kept in community aquariums with fishes totally unsuited to be their companions. Few fishes are more attractive to the novice than baby angelfish, and they are frequently purchased with others to occupy a receptacle of from two or three gallons upward without regard to the future potential size or disposition of either the angels or their companions.

Even some of the "community tank combinations" suggested in fish books do not work out well in practice, since some of the fishes which are suggested turn out to be fin-nippers at maturity and are not able to resist the long, trailing feelers of angelfish or the handsome filaments which are produced at the lower part of the anal fin and at the upper and lower lobe of the caudal fin or tail. While fin-nipping companions are not likely to be fatal to the angels, certainly they keep them from ever developing into the magnificent creatures which they are capable of becoming. Fast-swimming, active and playful carp-family fishes such as tiger barbs and rosy barbs have been suggested to occupy the same aquarium with large and medium angels, as have tetras like the blind cave tetra and *Moenkhausia* species and others which become sizable at maturity and are not averse to using their teeth on angelfish fins. A rather strangely disastrous companion for angelfish is one of their near look-alikes, *Monodactylus argenteus*, which will usually administer "hair cuts" to all the angelfish present almost as if the mono were attempting to make the angels conform to its own appearance by neatly clipping

The many popular different catfish species of the genus *Corydoras* are compatible tankmates for angels, because they present no danger at all of combativeness and in addition have a positive value in that their constant pacing of the bottom of the tank helps to swirl up organic matter so that it becomes more easily trapped by a filter. The species shown is *Corydoras aeneus*.

Tiger barbs are fast-moving fish that seem always to be in motion from one end of the tank to the other, and they have been known to nip many an enticingly long fin. Accordingly, they are not recommended as suitable tankmates for angelfish, even though they are not by any means the least suitable. Photo by R. Zukal.

off the top of the dorsal and bottom of the anal.

Better choices are large swordtails, thick-lipped gouramis, kissing gouramis, large mollies and fishes of similar nature. Certainly any of the little *Corydoras* catfishes are excellent choices, as well as their cousin, the emerald catfish *Brochis coeruleus*. Suckermouth catfishes such as *Loricaria* are also excellent; like *Corydoras* and *Brochis*, they help clean up uneaten scraps of food, but they also aid in controlling the growth of algae. Among the heavyweights of sucker catfishes such as the old favorite *Hypostomus plecostomus*, the eventual large size and sometimes the aggressiveness of a really large specimen make them perhaps a bit less suitable for an aquarium with angels than some of their smaller relatives. A good combination for an aquarium containing a heavy planting of substantial vegetation such as some of the larger species of *Sagittaria* would probably be *Cichlasoma festivum* and angelfish, since they are found together in nature.

Angelfish are often kept with discus to "keep the discus on their toes" by offering them a little competition at mealtime. Some discus breeders say this keeps discus appetites at their peak, and certainly the shapes and habits of the two are complementary to each other.

It would be impractical to attempt listing all the fishes which make desirable co-occupants with angelfish as opposed to those which do not. In the first place, experiences and circumstances vary. Generally speaking, however, fishes which are more serene and deliberate in their actions and non-aggressive but at the same time capable of taking care of themselves make the best candidates for consideration in a community containing angelfish. There is no question that angelfish do better in an aquarium all to themselves.

ANGELFISH AT HOME

In nature, wherever angelfishes of the various species are found, they are invariably found on whichever bank of the river is shallower. They are apparently never found under normal circumstances in midstream or on the deeper bank of the river. In Brazil this shallow side of the river which angels frequent is known as the *varje*, and during times of rain or high water on the river the *varje* is either totally or at least partially submerged. The angelfish are found near the shore, and only where there is vegetation.

Pterophyllum species can be observed often in the company of *Cichlasoma festivum* among growths of flooded cane when the river is up or among the roots of floating plants during low water periods. Observers have said that the *C. festivum* which accompany the angels are usually found ahead of or above them, almost as if they were doing scout duty. Water which angelfish frequent seldom seems to be more than six or seven feet deep. Dr. Axelrod, however, says *C. festivum* are almost universal in South American waters and the *C. festivum*/angelfish relationship is more legend than fact.

Spawning is early in the year when the water is high, flooding the bank and large areas of heavy vegetation. Numerous fishes of every sort are found in great numbers, and among them are many enemies. Baby angels are often found in small schools without the accompaniment of their parents, which have probably been driven away from their progeny.

One interesting observation of wild angels has been that although they are not easily captured during high water periods, they can be located by slapping the water's surface

A good choice of tankmates for angels might be *Cichlasoma festi-vum*, shown above.

Angelfish and discus (the discus species shown opposite is *Symph sodon aequifasciata axelrodi*) are "traditional" tank companions b cause they come from the same general region, but discus aren't rea good companions for any other fish. Putting angels into a tank hou ing discus might help the discus, which are abnormally temperame tal and illness-prone, but putting discus into a tank housing ang won't help the angels.

Dead angelfish lying by the banks of a Brazilian waterway in which they had lived; these fish were collected by poisoning the water. The fish are found in great number in their native waters.

with a canoe paddle. If there are angels present they reportedly leap out of the water. Even most aquarists have noticed how easily terrified angels can become, and in nature they are reportedly so sensitive to sudden sounds or motions made in the water that sometimes they will leap completely above the surface, fall flat on their sides and simply lie there quivering, apparently in such a state of shock that they will allow themselves to be picked up by hand. For this reason the Brazilian Indians have given them the rather dubious title of *pacu doido*, which means "crazy surface fish."*

---

*Dr. Axelrod says that this behavior is absolutely not typical of angelfish and that "pacu doido" derives from "pacu" meaning the *Metynnis* species and "doido" which means crazy. Axelrod has never heard of angelfish being called "pacu doido," but all cichlids are called "acara" and angelfish are sometimes called "acara bandeira" or "flag cichlid" by the Brazilian caboclo.

THE SPECIES OF ANGELFISH

The first freshwater angelfish known to science* was described in 1831 by Cuvier & Valenciennes in *Histoire Naturelle des Poissons*. They named the fish, which was described from a preserved specimen, *Platax scalaris*, since to them it appeared to be related to the batfishes of the marine genus *Platax*, which also have very tall and deep dorsal and anal fins.

Later, in 1839, the fish was renamed by Heckel when it was realized that it belonged to the family Cichlidae. The new name was *Pterophyllum scalare* (pronounced TER O FILL' UM SKA LAR'E.) As with many other scientific names, the meaning is interesting and quite descriptive. *Pterophyllum* means "winged leaf" and is derived from Greek, while *scalare* means "like a flight of stairs" in reference to the dorsal fin. It is a Latin word, and can also mean "ladder."

The first living angelfish were imported into Hamburg, Germany in 1911, and a short while later specimens reached the United States. Dr. George S. Myers recalled that when he first saw them in 1917 they were extremely scarce, and adult fish were selling at a price of $75 for two, with no guarantee of sex.

Finally they were spawned in Philadelphia, which in that time was considered by many to be the center of fish-keeping in the U.S., by a gentleman named Paullin. The prices, however, remained prohibitively high, although the aquarium-raised specimens quickly sold out.

In 1922 and 1923 there were large importations of angels to the U.S. from Germany, where breeders had been

---

* Not counting Lichtenstein's 1821 paper, which went unnoticed for many years; Lichtenstein described an angelfish under the name *Zeus scalaris.*

This is the first published color photograph of parent angelfish and their young. Published around 1935, it appeared in the aquarium literature of the day and probably had a significant influence in helping to popularize angelfish among aquarium hobbyists. The young angels shown were 65 days old at the time the photograph was taken.

This community tank holds angelfish and two individuals of the Asiatic cichlid species *Etroplus maculatus* as well as swordtails, *Xiphophorus helleri*. Although optimum conditions for the fishes involved are disparate, they do well enough together. The angels usually aren't bothered by the presence of the swordtails in their tank and probably would even benefit, because they'd be sure to gobble up any swordtail or other livebearer babies born in their tank.

successful in propagating them, and this brought the price in America down substantially. The greatly increased availability also resulted in breeding success in the U.S., further increasing availability.

About 1927 an angelfish called *Zwergscalare* (dwarf scalare) appeared in Germany; this fish had been imported from the Amazon. The importer's name was Eimeke, and in 1928 Dr. Ahl of the Berlin Museum described the fish as a new species, naming it *Pterophyllum eimekei* in honor of the importer.

Another angelfish, *Pterophyllum altum*, had been described from the upper Orinoco in Venezuela in 1903. This is the largest and deepest-bodied of the angels and has been occasionally imported in recent years. This is quite an impressive show fish, although it apparently has not been spawned in the aquarium.

The other species so far recorded was described as *Plataxoides dumerilii* by Castelnau in 1855. This fish as described had the shallower body which distinguishes *P. eimekei* from *P. scalare* and *P. altum* for the most part in appearance. It is known that the two fishes known as *Pterophyllum scalare* and *Pterophyllum eimekei* will interbreed and that the resulting offspring breed successfully. It may well be, and has been suggested, that the angelfish of the aquarium hobby today are for the most part a mixture of the two and that very few, if any, pure *P. scalare* or *P. eimekei* are kept by aquarists.

It has also been suggested that *P. eimekei* may not be a species distinct from *P. scalare*, but simply a variety or a subspecies. There also exists a possibility that *Pterophyllum dumerilii* and *P. eimekei* are the same species, since the body shape is so similar. This possibility further clouds the status of *P. eimekei*, since if they should prove to be the same, *Pterophyllum dumerilii* (Castelnau, 1855) would take

Angelfish in good health are an imposing sight, whether they're maintained in a mixed-species tank or by themselves.

Pterophyllum scalare in its most typical color pattern.

Pterophyllum altum.

precedence over the more familiar name *Pterophyllum eimekei* Ahl, 1928.

Following are descriptions of the angelfish species which have been seen in the aquarium as they are now understood.

Pterophyllum eimekei Ahl, 1928

Popular name: Angelfish, scalare; lesser angelfish
Range: Middle Amazon

For some time, *Pterophyllum eimekei* was considered to be the angelfish commonly found in the aquarium hobby and the easiest to breed.

The body depth is not as great as in *P. altum* or *P. scalare*, being found one-and-one-half times in the length from tip of snout to base of caudal fin. The front part of the lateral line is much flatter and less curved than in the other two species. The curve of the upper profile of the head is gentle and even, and there is no deep indentation between the snout and forehead. There are about thirty-two to thirty-four scales in a straight series from the upper part of the opercular slit to the caudal base, according to Myers. Sterba has the lateral line count at twenty-nine to thirty-six. Myers found *P. eimekei* to have only twenty-eight vertebrae, while both *P. scalare* and *P. altum* had thirty.

Coloration is silvery on the sides, with a bluish sheen. Upper part of back and nape blackish brown-yellow with small brownish-red blotches. Gill cover silver with shining green blotches. Several prominent black transverse bands on sides, the second, fourth and sixth being most intense while those between are rather obscure. There is also a band through the eye. The fourth and most prominent band runs from the tip of the dorsal to the tip of the anal. Ventral fins or "feelers" rather steel-blue at bases, bluish-white on extended portions. Posterior edge of ventrals blackish or dark.

The original importation of *Pterophyllum eimekei* was said to have come from the mouth of the Rio Negro near Manaos, Brazil.

Pterophyllum scalare (Lichtenstein, 1823)

Popular name: Angelfish, scalare
Range: Amazon to Guyana

Pterophyllum scalare is obviously the fish from which the popular name *scalare*, originated.

P. scalare has a greater body depth than *P. eimekei*, the greatest depth of the body fitting into the length from snout-tip to tail-root one-and-one-eighth to one-and-one-fourth times. According to Myers there are thirty-three to thirty-eight scales in a straight series from the upper end of the gill-slit to the end of the fleshy part of the caudal root, while according to Sterba there are thirty-eight to forty in the lateral line series.

Coloration is greenish-gray to olive gray, with a bright silvery sheen. Back brownish-olive with reddish-brown or yellowish cast. Sometimes a reddish-brown blotch in front of and below dorsal. Four prominent bands on sides with three shorter and less prominent bands between; all bands are black to dark gray, varying with conditions. The fifth band is darkest and boldest and reaches from the tip of the dorsal to the tip of the anal.

Pterophyllum altum Pellegrin, 1903

Popular name: Long-finned angelfish, deep angelfish
Range: Orinoco

The body of *Pterophyllum altum* is much deeper than that of either *P. scalare* or *P. eimekei*. The dorsal and anal fins have very long bases and are much longer than the other two species. The forehead angles up very sharply from the snout, which is strongly concave. The greatest body depth is equal to or greater than the distance from the tip of the snout to the end of the caudal root or tail

Pterophyllum dumerilii.

Opposite: *Pterophyllum altum* showing a brassy sheen over the body and fins; these specimens were imported by the well-known German commercial breeder Heiko Bleher.

A wild-caught *Pterophyllum scalare*; the speckles scattered over the fish's dorsum are very often present on wild angelfish.

root. The front part of the lateral line, which is in two parts, is more curved than in the other species. There are forty-one to forty-seven scales in a straight series from the upper end of the gill or opercular opening to the end of the caudal root.

Coloration is greenish gray to olive gray, with a bright silvery appearance. Several bold black bands on sides, the most prominent of which runs from the tip of the dorsal to the tip of the anal. Upper part of body with brown dots, a few brown to blackish blotches on flanks.

First described from specimens in Paris Museum which were from San Fernando de Atabapo, Upper Orinoco, Venezuela.

Pterophyllum dumerilii (Castelnau, 1855)

This species apparently has not been imported.

ANGELFISH VARIETIES

Nature is constantly striving to improve her products, apparently never satisfied that "perfection" has been achieved. Through a system of trial and error, mutations, or those creatures which differ in some way from normal stock of their kind, are produced. Sometimes the resulting product is a hopeless disaster without a chance for survival, like a fish with two heads or five eyes. At other times milder forms of mutation occur, such as albino or black angelfish. Perhaps they survive. In nature, once in a great while, the true purpose will be served and a mutation will be produced which can run faster, climb higher, dig deeper or swim better than its predecessors, and if more than one are produced within an ecological niche to which they are unusually well adapted and which they efficiently and successfully fill, and they reproduce, evolution has taken place.

Most mutations are lost in nature. Not all are even remotely functional, and many which are functional fail to survive simply because they are "different." Some are weak, others are only poorly adapted to their circumstances. While nature has no time for such folly, the aquarist can intervene when a desirable mutation or a fish which is "different" appears among an otherwise normal spawning. The aquarist can give the creature added protection and attention and perhaps later breed it selectively to establish its form.

With angelfish as with guppies, although certainly to a lesser degree, a number of handsome and desirable strains have been developed. These varieties have become established in our aquaria, and several have had substantial impact upon the hobby of aquarium keeping.

Opposite is a fish showing the normal regular color pattern of *Pterophyllum scalare*; above are representatives of the color variety called zebra angels, developed in the early 1970's.

Black Lace Angelfish

Black lace angels are the steppingstones to the solid black variety. The primary difference in black lace and ordinary angels is in the intensity of the pattern, which on the fins, especially, takes on a decidedly lace-like effect. They are beautiful fish in their own right, being in the opinion of some among the most handsome of angels. The fact that they have been too often publicized as being "black angels which didn't turn out" has relegated them to an undeservedly low position on the angelfish totem pole. There are few more beautiful fishes than a mature pair of well cared-for black lace angels.

A mating of two black lace parents produces 25% black, 50% black lace and 25% silver or ordinary angels. Unfortunately, the blacks are less robust than either their black lace or silver brethren. Fewer of them survive to free-swimming, and even those which do respond very favorably to early separation from their more vigorous litter-mates. This is not difficult even at an early age if hatching has taken place in a gallon jar or similar receptacle, since their darker pigmentation is easily seen. Because of their relative delicacy, temperature stability is especially important during hatching, pre-swimming and early free-swimming days of blacks.

Black lace, which is quite a hardy strain, has been combined with other varieties such as veil, marble and even blushing, and a new strain with even more color has been called the "zebra angel."

Black Angelfish

Certainly the most striking and, in the opinion of many, the most handsome of *Pterophyllum* color varieties is the beautiful solid black angelfish. Few aquarium fishes are better show-stoppers than a perfect mature pair of these magnificent creatures in a tastefully arranged aquarium. Almost like voids of utter darkness against the aquarium background, their velvet black bodies still seem a bit fantastic, even to hobbyists who have been exposed to them for many years. Somehow, above all the others, their melanistic purity and freedom from frills seem to denote that quality of grace, dignity and a number of other essences which through lack of a really proper and fitting term we often end up referring to as real "class."

Black angelfish apparently first appeared in the United States at the Florida fish farm of H. Woolfe in the early 1950's. These original fish were supposedly from Germany. While their distribution is not completely clear, it was in 1955 that black angelfish seemed to turn up in a number of widely scattered places at the same time.

In the June, 1955 issue of *Tropical Fish Hobbyist* was an article on breeding black angels in which Mr. and Mrs. Fred Ludwig described their success. In July, 1955 came

Young black angels developed by Mr. and Mrs. Fred Ludwig.

A black lace veil angelfish.

Black angels.

articles in both *The Aquarium* and *Aquarium Journal* concerning black angelfish. The article in *The Aquarium*, by Dr. William T. Innes, pointed out several people who had black angels in such places as Philadelphia, Corning, New York, Robertson, Missouri and California, while the *Aquarium Journal* mentioned fish which had been raised by Mr. James Ellis of North Hollywood, California. Dr. Innes pointed out differences in what he called the "style" of the several strains of blacks he had seen or seen pictured, and the point was well illustrated with photographs of fish owned by Mr. and Mrs. Mahlon Griffin of Corning, N.Y., Mr. Joe Berkowitz of Philadelphia and Mr. Ellis of North Hollywood. At least two of the strains seem to have appeared spontaneously from what seemed to be "normal" stock.

Black angels can be produced in several ways. Matings of two black lace parents will produce approximately 25% black, 50% black lace and 25% silver. Matings of a black and a black lace will produce 50% black and 50% black lace. Matings of two blacks produce 100% black. A black and a silver mating results in no blacks, only black lace. Almost all blacks result from black lace.

Half-black angels originated in Holland in the early 1950's. They disappeared for a while and then showed up again in 1968–1969 in Singapore. For some odd reason they have never become popular.

Veiltail Angelfish

Veiltail angels, as the name implies, have extraordinarily long, veil-like tails. In addition, the other fins are also longer and larger than they would normally be.

The silver veiltail, which is the counterpart of the ordinary silver angelfish except for its long finnage, is colored in the same pattern as the common or silver angelfish. This long-finned variety first appeared as a single fish in a spawning of ordinary angels by a Mr. Buschendorf in

Half-black angel.

Germany in 1956. It was introduced into America by Mr. Bill Sternke of Sunnyland Fish Farms in Florida.

The veiltail characteristic is dominant, and if a veil angel [*] is crossed with a silver, the results will be 50% veil and 50% silver. A mating of two veils produces 25% ordinary angels, 50% veils and 25% long-tailed veils[**] which have even longer fins than the ordinary veiltails. The latter reproduce 100% true when bred together, but spawns are not as large as with the regular veil, and the young of this "super veil" seem less robust. The finnage of some veils is so long that the dorsal becomes easily broken or at least "bent," making it difficult for the fish to hold it erect.

Veiltails are very peaceful and undemanding as well as easy to breed. There are a number of color varieties of veiltail also available incorporating most of the colors and patterns found in normally-finned fish.

[*] heterozygous condition

[**] homozygous condition

Veiltail angels with highly drawn out fins have been available for a long time and are available in many different color varieties of angelfish. Above is a veiltail specimen of a marbled angel, and opposite is a veiltail of the regular (silver) variety.

Marble Angelfish

Marble angels, instead of having the ordinary black bars contrasting with the more or less silvery background pattern, have a very broken and non-uniform pattern of black and silver which certainly is well described as "marbled" or "marble." Dorsal and anal have black and white rays, while the pattern on the sides is quite and unpredictably broken from specimen to specimen. The caudal or tail is also unusually streaked with black. The over-all impression of the fish at maturity is that they have been randomly but quite artistically adorned with black on white. In the head and back region there are often undertones of golden, and in certain lighting there are traces of greenish and blue. There are lighter as well as darker versions of the marble angel, and both are quite handsome creatures which are difficult to describe, since they are much more impressive in person than words or photographs indicate.

The marble pattern when crossed with black lace produces some babies which appear black when young but later prove actually to be black lace marble, expressing both characteristics in the same fish. This has been described as looking like black lace with some extra marking in what ordinarily are areas light in the lace pattern. When crossed with other color variations such as blushing or silver, some marble angels are produced.

The marble pattern as we know it today was developed by Mr. Charles A. Ash of San Bernardino, California; the first marble angels appeared on the market in 1968.

In 1963 commercial breeder Bud Goddard, working in Lakeland, Florida, discovered two different aberrant angelfish sports in different batches of normal angelfish fry. One was an albino, and the other was a fish with a strange pattern of irregular white streakings on a dark background. This latter fish was called marbleized because of its pattern; earnest attempts were made by Goddard to perpetuate the sport, but the attempts failed, even though the fish produced at least two separate generations of fry, after first being mated to a black lace angel and then to fry produced in the marbleized/black lace mating. The albino, a male, was blind and failed to fertilize eggs produced during its matings, so it too died out.

Golden Angelfish

The golden angel was developed from a single runty little individual which appeared among the thousands of angelfish which Mr. Carl Naja of Milwaukee was raising commercially around 1963. So unspectacular was the little fish that it was almost discarded, but it was placed in an aquarium by itself and for a time was forgotten.

In the few weeks alone the fish grew very rapidly but developed a blotchy appearance which made it look as if it were diseased. After a few more weeks alone, the fish turned completely yellow. After special pampering and care, the fish was bred back to normal angels, producing only normal-appearing offspring. Finally, after breeding the fish, a male, back to his daughters, six young golden angels were discovered among the thousands of fry produced. Unfortunately, it took six to nine months for the fish to turn gold. Years of development improved this situation, and when the fish were first marketed in 1969 they could be expected to turn golden in about three months, until which time they are rather mottled in appearance.

From this same stock, which was originally black lace, Mr. Naja also reportedly was getting some albinos. Strangely, the pigmentation of the eyes on these albino fish changed from black to red only as the fish aged.

Another golden angelfish strain was produced in Hong Kong by Peter Wong in the early 1970's.

Blushing Angelfish

Blushing angels have a red cheek area and no pattern of

Juvenile marble angelfish.

This is the marble or marbleized angelfish developed by commercial breeder Bud Goddard in 1963; it predated the marbled angels developed by Charles Ash in 1968 but died out as a strain.

Black lace veil angel.

stripes on the body. While the dorsal and anal fins are outlined in black, for the most part they can be described as being almost plain and unpatterned. The reddish cheek area, for which the name "blushing" was given, is somewhat variable in size.

Various crossing procedures have resulted in patterns such as marble blushing, black lace blushing and veiltail blushing.

Blushing angels are reportedly among the most delicate of angel fish types. The blushing angel or "Conles blushing angelfish" was produced by Mr. Lester Boisvert of Connecticut.

BREEDING ANGELFISH

Few tropical fishes have had as much written about their breeding as angelfish. For years they were considered to be "problem fish," sharing a rather exclusive niche with neon tetras, red rasboras and several other fishes with which consistent success was notoriously difficult. Fortunately, the onslaught of time and the efforts of skilled breeders have produced not only aquarium-raised stock which is more readily breedable in several of these species, but also techniques which have made their successful propagation almost predictable. The angelfish is one of these, and success can be expected by anyone willing to follow a few basic procedures.

Selecting The Breeders

There are three ways to obtain a breeding pair of angels; buy a pair which has already spawned and produced fertile eggs, buy a number of angels and wait for them to pair off, or attempt to select a pair from a number of large angels, using your own judgment in sexing them.

Mated pairs of angelfish have always been relatively expensive. The price increases according to color and finnage characteristics as well as the size and condition of the pair. Larger fish produce more eggs and are therefore more financially rewarding to a breeder. Silver angels, although they could be considered among the common aquarium fishes, are also among those perennial best sellers which are known in the aquarium trade as "bread and butter fish." There is always a demand for them, and although the going wholesale price, which is what the breeder can expect to receive, may at times be rather low, a producing pair can continually turn out salable fish.

Veiltail gold blushing angel developed by John Gonzalez of Ed's Tropical Aquarium.

The blushing angel developed by Lester Boisvert.

Young gold angels of the Carl Naja strain.

Depending on age, size and quality, silver angels can be purchased in mated pairs at prices ranging from $10 (£4) to $25 (£10). This, of course, is subject to availability, and at times it may be very difficult to obtain a mated pair of fish.

The second alternative, buying several and allowing them to select their own mates, is not only less expensive but also likely to produce more than one pair of mated breeders. If this method is chosen, you can buy either young, inexpensive fish or larger, almost mature fish. The older fish will be more expensive but have the advantage of reducing the period of time you must wait before they pair.

Without going into mathematics, a minimum of six fish should be selected, since the probability of obtaining a pair from six fish is very high, almost a "sure thing." If more are included, of course the odds go up. A consideration here, however, is that the more fish you have the more room you will need to grow them quickly and bring out their best potential.

When selecting your potential breeding stock, look for strong, robust and active fish. Choose individuals which are active feeders, especially, since this produces quick growth and a subsequent high rate of egg production in the females. Look for long, healthy fins and good contrast in color. Avoid individuals whose opercular covers or gill covers do not completely cover the opercular opening as they should, since this often means that the fish has been stunted by overcrowding. Such deficiencies could also indicate genetic qualities which would not be desirable to perpetuate. I have known of entire spawns of angelfish which have developed such deformities as having one operculum completely covering the opening while the other was shorter and did not, or having one ventral fin (feeler) longer than the other. Such physical defects, of course, make the fish worthless for sale to most potential buyers, and such fish certainly should not be used as breeders.

If your plans for breeding involve a variety other than the ordinary silver angel, select your potential breeders not only for the foregoing attributes (excluding color) but also for strongly showing the characteristics of the particular variety. Black lace should be dark and heavily patterned, with fins which are worthy of the name. Blacks should be jet-black, without little hints of silver peeping through. Veils should have long, untorn fins, and golds should have as little pattern as possible. This is also true of blushing angels which should also have the red opercular area for which they received their name, as large as possible. Primary to keep in mind is that *quality* begets *quality*. Silk purses are not produced from matings of sows' ears.

Sexing Angelfish

It has been said that only angelfish can accurately sex angelfish. This is not entirely true, although I would imagine their batting average to be somewhat better than that of even the most proficient angelfish breeder who has learned through experience to pick pairs of potential breeders from a group of fish. The fact is that angelfish *can* be sexed with a high degree of accuracy by certain breeders. The problem is in attempting to relate to others just how they do it, since most of those whom I have known who are really good at pair selection do it at least partially by "feel." There are a few physical indications which have been suggested which may be helpful to those who would like to try picking a pair.

One indication which has often been noted is the apparent difference in the distance between the ventral fins and the beginning of the anal fin. This distance is greater in the female.

One of the more interesting suggested ways of sexing

Bud Goddard's albino angel; this fish was blind and did not reproduce itself.

This black, silver and reddish-gold sport was discovered among a large group of black lace angels bred at Lakeland Fish Hatcheries in Florida, around 1966; it is similar in pattern to angels that show up from time to time among populations of gold angels.

angelfish is similar to "candling" eggs. The procedure involves cutting a one-inch circle out of a piece of cardboard, placing the hole near the side of the fish to be sexed and projecting a bright light through the fish's body from the opposite side. Using the cardboard as a shade and concentrating on the area at eye level and directly above the vent, a light area can be observed which is said to be somewhat pear-shaped in the male and rather oval-shaped in the female. The vent of the female is said to be more prominent than that of the male, even at times when the breeding tubes are not apparent. When the breeding tubes or genital papillae are in evidence, the female's is larger and projects slightly backward, while the male's is carried at an angle closer to the vertical.

The anterior edge of the anal fin joins the belly of the female in a slightly straighter line than in the male. In other words, the fin and body join at a sharper, more noticeable angle in the case of the male.

My own personally preferred method may seem the least likely to some. Instead of scrutinizing very closely, the fish are observed from at least eight or ten feet away. It is necessary to have a reasonable amount of light entering the aquarium from the front so that the light will reflect from the sides of the fish. The sides of mature and well-conditioned males will appear quite flattened in comparison to those of mature, well-conditioned females, in which a slight abdominal bulge will show at certain angles of the reflected light. The reflected light actually makes the female look plumper. Several fish should be present in the aquarium for comparison, since the difference is more noticeable in some individuals than in others. The group should be watched long enough to develop definite impressions of the observed individuals as their movements change the angles of reflected light.

Mature females are generally a bit thicker or broader before feeding when viewed from above.

There are numerous other breeder-suggested ways of sexing angelfish. Included here are only those which I consider of possible value to the average aquarist on a practical basis. Practically speaking, there is no crystal ball formula. Any clairvoyance concerning the ability to determine the gender of angels by simply observing them is most likely due more to experience than to mystic capability.

Tank Requirements For Breeding

While angelfish which are in breeding condition can be bred in an aquarium as small as ten gallons, or on rare occasions even smaller, this in my opinion is not a good situation for any but temporary housing for a breeding pair. In an aquarium of such size, sooner or later domestic problems arise even among what to all appearances are a most compatible pair. I would suggest a minimum of fifteen gallons in which to house or breed a mature pair of angels, and if you plan not to remove the eggs from the parents to be hatched separately, a larger aquarium will be required. Pairs which are intended to raise and care for their own offspring, which still has to be one of the most glorious and heartwarming experiences in fishkeeping, should have a minimum of twenty-five gallon capacity, or larger if possible. There are several reasons for this.

Obviously a pair of fully grown angelfish shepherding a flock of perhaps two or three hundred offspring would be extremely crowded in a lesser container, especially when the youngsters started to grow. Secondly, the larger the aquarium, the less easily disturbed the breeders are, and this is *most* important, since easily disturbed angels are very prone to eating either their eggs or babies. Larger aquariums seem to give them a much greater sense of security and tremendously increase your chances of having them successfully rear a family. Not only will a 45- or 50-gallon tank proportionately decrease chances of

Angels have come almost traditionally to be linked with various of the Amazon swordplants (genus *Echinodorus*) almost in the same way that guppies have come to be linked with water sprite (*Ceratopteris*), probably because most spawnings while the fish was still relatively little known occurred on swordplants. The angels really have no specific plant preferences and in many cases are shown off to better advantage in tanks in which the main vegetative emphasis is on tall, thin-bladed plants like *Vallisneria* and *Sagittaria* rather than on the relatively broad-bladed popular swordplants. *Echinodorus* and *Aponogeton* species are the major plants shown here.

Strata for receiving the eggs of angels vary from the natural such as the egg-laden *Echinodorus* leaf shown below to the contrived, such as the piece of slate supported on a wire base, as shown above. The slate shown holding the eggs of the golden angels (Peter Wong strain) is inclined much less steeply than most artificial egg deposit surfaces.

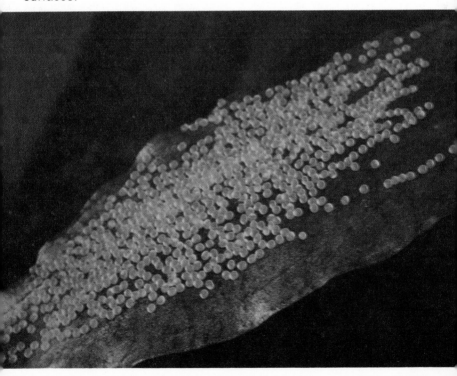

lunching on caviar or later their own progeny, the babies can be allowed to stay with their parents for a much longer time before overcrowding becomes a problem. Larger aquariums are not nearly as subject to pollution or chemical buildup due to waste, etc. This is perhaps the most important factor in dealing successfully with angelfish: water freshness. This is discussed in more detail elsewhere in the book.

Aquarium Size For Raising Potential Breeders

While the foregoing was concerned with breeding quarters for already established pairs, those who intend to grow their own breeders must also consider the size of the aquarium in which these fish will be tenanted. Since growth is one of the main considerations, as much room as possible should be given to the several fish from which it is your hope and intention that at least one pair will select each other. Although the probability of obtaining one or more pairs increases with more individuals, it is probably wise to limit the number of your potential breeding stock to eight or ten individuals. More than this will reduce the area per fish significantly in all but a very large aquarium; also, it is easier to keep prime foods provided and the water in top condition if the aquarium is relatively uncrowded. More fish require more food, which in turn creates more solid and dissolved waste, and causes a necessary increase in the number of cleanings and partial water changes which must be performed to insure fastest growth and best appetites in the fish. Again, a 25-gallon aquarium would seem to be a minimum unless the fish are to be started in a smaller one and moved to larger quarters as their size demands it. There will be those who disagree and who have raised breeding-size angels in smaller aquariums, but this is intended to be an outline for minimum optimum conditions which should assure you not only a good chance of success but also high quality stock either for your own pleasure or for selling.

Although I do not consider angelfish to be particularly good community aquarium fish under many situations, probably as many pairs find each other in a community aquarium where they have been raised with other fishes and perhaps other angels as under any other circumstances. Actually, for the would-be breeder with space too limited to furnish his potential breeding stock with a large aquarium of their own, raising a few angels in a large community aquarium until breeding occurs between a pair can be a very workable solution. Some successful angelfish breeders even continue to leave the pair in the community situation, removing the eggs when they spawn to be hatched elsewhere. (More on how this is done a bit later.) Essentially, if you are starting with immature or unmated angels in hopes of producing a working pair, place them where they will get the most room, the best food and the cleanest conditions you can offer them.

Aquarium Arrangement

For the most serious-minded breeder who is willing to forego certain aesthetic qualities for the sake of production, a bare aquarium has certain advantages over one which is planted and in which the aquarium floor is covered with the conventional layer of gravel. First, there is less danger of uneaten food or other pollutant materials having even a slight chance to accumulate without being observed. Another advantage is that the bare aquarium is easier to keep spotlessly clean, both through filtration and other cleaning processes such as siphoning debris periodically from the bottom. This serves the dual purpose of partially removing and replacing a portion of the water on a regular basis, a procedure which cannot be too strongly recommended and which virtually all consistently successful discus breeders adhere to religiously. The reason for the mention of discus, which may seem strange in an angelfish book, is that care and breeding for *Symphysodon* (discus) and

Depending entirely upon personal taste and the use to which the aquarium will be put, an angel tank can range anywhere from heavily planted (above) to completely bare. (opposite). Although the fish might derive a heightened sense of security from a planted tank, the plants offer no great utilitarian advantages.

Pterophyllum are basically the same, with discus being notoriously more touchy. Treated with care such as their more expensive pancake-shaped relatives would receive, angelfish respond fantastically well, and although angelfish are less demanding there is reward in the satisfaction that you have offered them the best of care.

While some breeders use potted plants in their bare breeding aquariums, such as large *Cryptocorynes* or Amazon swords (*Echinodorus*), moving or removing the plants for cleaning procedures, others prefer the amazingly lifelike non-toxic plastic plants which are designed and produced for aquarium use by several manufacturers. Broad-leaved varieties should be chosen, such as those simulating Amazon swords. Although such plants will somewhat improve the appearance of the breeding aquarium, this is not their primary purpose, which is that of a spawning receptacle, since angelfish show a natural preference for spawning on broad-leaved plants. Professional breeders have for years circumvented the inconvenience and other minor disadvantages associated with providing live plants for angels to spawn upon by using such items as strips of slate or glass tubes painted green inside with some sort of non-toxic paint. In both cases these were usually mounted in a base of cement or some other substance so that they could be made to stand upright. Strips of slate, however, are sometimes merely leaned against the side of the aquarium at an almost upright angle. When any of the foregoing are used to receive the spawn of breeding angelfish the eggs can either be left with the parents or easily removed to be hatched separately according to the choice of the aquarist.

For the aquarist who is less intent on sheer production, but wishes to partake of the almost incomparable experience of watching his breeders go through the entire procedure of spawning and raising their offspring into an assemblage of miniatures of themselves, protecting them

In this spawning, the parents chose the vertically inclined, roughly rectangular piece of slate to deposit the eggs even though there were many fairly broad-leafed plants that could have served the purpose.

The male (at left) and female angel hover near the place they have chosen to deposit the eggs. At this point all of the preliminary skirmishing has been accomplished, and the fish are almost ready to settle down to the site-cleaning and spawning proper.

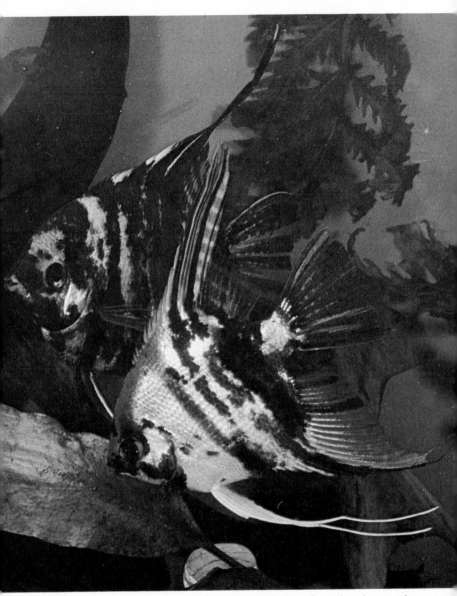

While the male hovers in the background, the female cleans the leaf. In angelfish spawnings, the egg site is most usually cleaned meticulously; in most cases, both parents take part in cleaning the area, but in some cases only one parent does the job.

Regardless of their color or finnage differences, the major varieties of a given angelfish species freely interbreed. Here a veiltail of the normal silver pattern and a black lace with normal finnage care for their eggs.

in infancy, bedding them down at night and generally ushering them through the first days of life while showing them the ropes of living, either the "bare aquarium" approach can be used or the admittedly more aesthetically satisfying "natural" approach utilizing a furnished aquarium. The phrase "furnished aquarium" in this case is meant to be taken in a broad sense, according to one's own personal tastes and preferences; it could be considered to be loosely synonymous with "decorated aquarium." To the purist, this might strictly mean an aquarium with actively growing and thriving plants, natural rocks and other objects which could conceivably be found in nature. To the decorator who feels that for his particular purposes he can improve on nature, plastic plants and stone pagodas may be more suitable, and some may even prefer a combination of the two. Any of these can be used effectively, although I recommend that a minimum number of solid

A newly hatched angelfish is being spit back among its brothers and sisters into the plant mass to which the parent angelfish have transferred them from the spawning site. What appear to be very small ramshorn snails among the leaves of the plant actually are the eyes of the young angels.

The spawning has progressed to the point that many eggs have already been laid on a *Cryptocoryne* leaf; here the male angelfish is fertilizing the string of eggs just laid by the female standing by.

Here the male has taken up a position by the *Cryptocoryne* leaf as the female extrudes a new string of eggs; as soon as she departs from the leaf, he will fertilize the eggs she has laid.

objects such as rocks or the aforementioned manmade artifacts under which waste can accumulate be used. Again, your own judgment is your guide, and although I have my own personal opinions which lean at least toward reasonably natural appearances, it is not the purpose of this book or even my wish to impose these upon you, but to give guidelines which should steer you toward success within the bounds of your own preferred physical arrangements of the tank.

If a naturally arranged or otherwise decorated aquarium is to be used, several things must be kept in mind concerning cleanliness, which is tremendously important. An aquarium containing gravel is more subject to organic pollution from uneaten food, waste, etc., that collects

Many different types of siphons and other removers of aquarium debris are offered by fish supply dealers. All, even the power-operated types, are relatively inexpensive and are handy aquarium accessories.

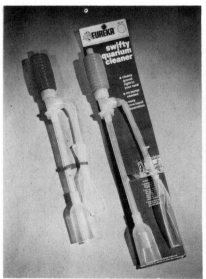

there undetected. The worst form of this trouble occurs when the organic matter in the sand causes it to turn black in spots, usually under a rock or other solid object, which can even consist of the base used to hold a plastic plant in the sand. Under these circumstances hydrogen sulfide gas ("rotten egg" gas) and other pollutants are produced, and can be disastrous. Depending on filtration, this can even happen while the water remains perfectly clear. Frequent siphoning of the bottom or very rapid filtration from a power filter or a fast outside filter helps avoid the buildup of waste which usually leads to this. One of the most valuable tools in aquarium keeping which is particularly applicable here is the aquarium "vacuum cleaner." Several models are available from various manufacturers, but the one I prefer consists of a large-diameter clear plastic tube which is closed at one end except for a small diameter hole. The small hole is covered with a rubber flap which serves as a valve, and a large squeeze bulb with a hose attached fits over the end of the plastic tube. When the bulb is squeezed, water is drawn upward and pushed out the hose. Although the device comes equipped with little cloth filter bags which are to be tied on the end of the hose in order to trap detritus which is pumped up while letting the water pass through and back into the aquarium, the hose can instead be extended in order to simply siphon out water, detritus and all. The vacuum cleaner cleans *beneath* the sand, since the restricted flow of the small hose draws the sand only partially up the larger tube so that only the lighter debris is removed while the weight of the sand returns it to the bottom. In this way the sand can be thoroughly cleaned while at the same time water is removed for replacement.

Aquarium Location

The best location for an angelfish breeding aquarium is a quiet one. It should be relatively free of both traffic and

Above: young gold angels at two weeks of age. Below: considerably older, these angels, although still very young, are greatly advanced in development.

Angelfish fry surround their parents; the fry shown here are free-swimming and can actively forage for their food, but they have not yet progressed to the point of being immediately recognizable as angelfish.

noise and should have no bright lighting across from it which would create shadows when there is activity near the tank. To fishes, passing shadows as often as not mean the presence of predators, and most become frightened and nervous when they are subjected to moving shadows. Nervous or frightened fishes seldom are good breeders, and especially if an attempt is to be made to let the parents raise their offspring, freedom from disturbing elements is tremendously important.

Water Quality

Water quality, I feel, is often overemphasized in its importance. Most water is generally suitable for breeding most fishes, and unless ordinary tap water is extreme in pH or hardness it is usually best not to tamper with it. Angelfish have been raised and successfully bred under a wide range of water conditions. Certainly if water is around neutral in pH and no more than slightly hard it should be suitable in most cases.

As most aquarists know, pH is simply a term of reference within the boundaries of which the relative acidity or alkalinity of a substance can be indicated in terms of numbers ranging from 0 to 14, with 7 indicating neutral. Anything less than 7 is acid while anything more than 7 is alkaline. In other words, water which after testing is determined to have a pH of 6.8 is slightly acid; water with a pH of 7.2 is slightly alkaline. Aquarium test kits are available in various price ranges for testing pH, none of which is extremely expensive.

Hardness of water, on the other hand, is based upon the amount of dissolved salts of calcium and magnesium which are contained in the water. The presence of these substances directly affects the sudsing or lathering ability of soap in the water as well as affecting the health and reproduction of certain fishes. Depending on the nature of the calcium and magnesium compounds which are

Water hardness test kits and pH test kits are available at pet supply dealers everywhere, either separately or in combination units.

present, hardness can be either temporary, which means it will precipitate out with boiling, or permanent, which means it will stay in solution even when boiled. Both kinds of hardness are usually present in hard water, but boiling and carefully pouring off the upper two-thirds or so of the water for use will often reduce the hardness even if not eliminating it completely. Like pH kits, hardness test kits are also available, although your local water department can give you the exact hardness of your local water on any given day. They can also give you the pH, but this can change considerably after only a few days in an aquarium. Hardness test kits are more expensive than pH kits.

If your water should test between pH 6.8 and 7.2 with hardness less than 100 ppm (parts per million), consider it very good for breeding angels, almost ideal. Even in water outside these boundaries thousands and thousands of angels have been raised successfully. Ask your dealer

and some of the local aquarists at your aquarium society who are successful angel breeders about the suitability of unaltered tap water from your area for breeding angels.

Water which has been softened in a commercially available household water softening unit is perfectly suitable for use in aquariums. There are also small water softening "pillows" available from your dealer which can be placed in an aquarium filter to soften the water. These operate in the same manner as the larger household units, removing calcium and magnesium salts and replacing them with sodium salts. The process is known as "ion exchange."

One thing which must be remembered if water for your angelfish is such that you feel it must be altered in pH or in hardness: don't make rapid adjustments of this sort in the aquarium with the fish. Water should if possible instead be adjusted externally and used to replace the aquarium water with several partial changes unless adjustments are made slowly.

Spawning

One sure-fire sign of an imminent spawning is the appearance of the pair's *genital papillae*, little nipple-like structures which are often referred to as *ovipositors*, a word which literally means "egg-placer(s)." The genital papilla or ovipositor of the female usually appears first and in any case is more noticeable because it is larger and more blunt, while that of the male is more slender and pointed. These small protuberances which appear at the vent are used respectively for depositing the eggs and fertilizing them.

Half-black blushing angel. Most angelfish varieties are equally hardy and can be given the same basic treatment, although the long-finned forms require more attention to tank conditions that would have a tendency to hurt their finnage because of its length.

There are unconfirmed reports that in the true *Ptero-phyllum scalare* these breeding tubes are quite similar in both male and female. With angelfish commonly seen in the trade, however, which many authorities recognize as either *P. scalare* or a possible hybrid of *P. eimekei* and *P. scalare*, the obvious differences in the size and shape of the genital papillae is the first completely reliable indication of sex.

The extended genital papilla of the angelfish shown broadside in this photo marks its bearer as a female; a male's sperm tube would be shorter and more pointed.

Usually two or three days before spawning, the pair selects and begins scrupulously cleaning the spawning site, using their mouths to bite and scrub the surface of the leaf, slate or whatever has been chosen until they are satisfied with the condition of the object. The breeding tubes are visible at this time, but will become much more prominent just before spawning.

When the cleanliness of the spawning site has progressed to the point that it is beginning to meet the approval of the prospective parents, the female will begin making a few test runs over the surface, neatly retracting her ventral fins or feelers along the lower sides of her abdomen and orienting her anal fin rearward so that as the fish "scoots" along the spawning surface a relatively straight line is formed by the entire underside, allowing the ovipositor to touch the leaf, slate or other surface without strain or restriction. The male soon takes a few passes at the site also, and after the pair has made a few dry runs and found everything in order, actual spawning commences. This time, as the female passes over the site, eggs are deposited which adhere to the surface. Alternating spawning runs with her, the male follows in the same ritual position which also allows him to press close to the spawn as he releases his milt or spermatozoa, fertilizing the eggs.

When spawning has been completed, there may be several hundred eggs or more, depending on the size of the female and her condition previous to egg-laying. The fish continue to take alternate turns passing over the eggs, and without close observation it may appear that spawning is continuing for some time after it has actually ceased. The continuing movements of the angels over the eggs serve the purpose of creating circulation through fanning movements of the pectoral fins. Infertile eggs, some of which turn white within hours of spawning, are removed by the parent fish, and while one fish is tending the eggs the other, often the male, is nearby standing guard duty,

Opposite and above: stages in egg decomposition and eventual fungusing. Opposite, above, parent angels are still depositing eggs. At this point, no egg has fungused. Opposite, below: Many of the eggs have started to go bad, either because they were unfertilized or because of some other defect in them. The starkly white eggs on the leaf are the bad ones. Above: all of the bad eggs on the leaf have been attacked by a fungus, visible as the fuzzy growth emanating from the eggs.

intercepting any would-be intruder, including the hand of the aquarist.

After you are sure that spawning has been completed, the final decision must be made, if it has not already been determined, as to whether the eggs will be left with the parents or removed and hatched separately. From an aesthetic point of view, and if you enjoy a challenge, the first idea may interest you more than the more productive alternative. The witnessing of any cichlid pairing, mating and raising of their offspring is a tremendous lesson in parental indulgence and patience, and certainly angelfish are more thrilling and more beautiful to watch in their assumption of parental duties than most.

On the other hand, they can prove quite temperamental, turning from loving, dedicated parents to infanticidal cannibals in a matter of minutes if circumstances are not to their liking. With exceptionally nervous or easily frightened pairs it is often best to remove the eggs so that they cannot be eaten. If you wish to let the parents raise the babies, it is best to make the attempt with a more stable pair.

Parental Care and Raising

If parents and eggs are left together, it is best to maintain as much quiet and freedom from traffic in the immediate area of the breeding aquarium as possible. Otherwise, treat the fish as you normally would. Some aquarists go so far as to cover the aquarium with paper or black plastic, using "peep holes" to observe the fish. This is not necessary and can cause more disturbance than it saves, since the fish have no warning before the reflector or top is suddenly lifted for food to be introduced or when circumstances otherwise call for entry into the aquarium.

An excellent system of filtration for the breeding aquarium is one of the several models available of what I call a "sponge filter." These are among the filters

Angelfish are not among the most aggressive of aquarium fishes, but they do have squabbles both among themselves and with fishes of other species. Spawning pairs often precede egg-laying with a stylized ritual of attack and retreat that often is considered as simple aggression.

Undergravel filter.

ordinarily classed as "biological filters," which means that they utilize living organisms which colonize within the filter and which break down the organic solid wastes of fishes, snails, etc., into less harmful and less unsightly substances. Properly utilized and not overworked, a biological filter can theoretically "consume" waste as it is produced, leaving the water fresh and sparkling without ever actually having to remove waste from the aquarium. The sponge-type biological filter consists of a piece of urethane or other synthetic sponge which has very many small pores. The pores are interconnected, and water can be drawn through the sponge at the center by means of an airlift of one kind or another. Dirt or waste is drawn to the outer edges of the sponge, and soon the colonies of organisms which were mentioned previously begin to form there and actually consume the unwanted material. The water is aerated by the bubbling of the airlift, it stays clear and free of practically all suspended matter which ordinary filters remove, and because of the small size of the pores in the sponge there is no danger of the baby angelfish becoming trapped in the filter. Living foods such as baby brine shrimp are also able to avoid the entrapment which is unavoidable with conventional filters unless they are turned off during feeding.

Undergravel filters, which also work biologically, are less desirable in this particular situation in my opinion. It is more difficult to clean an overworked and overloaded undergravel filtration system, since the sponge filter can simply be lifted out, rinsed and wrung out a couple of times and it is ready to go back to work. It is also completely effective in an otherwise bare aquarium. An undergravel filter can completely obscure a number of unhealthy conditions in an aquarium, especially when overfeeding occurs, since the water may remain clear even while the sand or gravel is foul below the filter. Cleaning presents its difficulties, and since a bare aquarium or one with the bottom just barely covered with sand for appearance allows the tank to be kept scrupulously clean without much effort, the sponge filter seems a better choice.

Depending on temperature, the eggs may hatch in about 36 to 48 hours. Before this time you may occasionally see an egg fall from the slate or leaf to which it is attached; one of the parents will make a dive for it, catching it in its mouth, swimming back to the spawning site and "spitting" the egg back into place with the others. Also you may notice one of the parents upon occasion removing an egg from the mass, picking it off and apparently eating it. Don't panic; this is simply the normal sanitary procedure of removing infertile or fungused eggs so that they won't endanger the whole spawn by possibly spreading fungus to the good eggs. Begin to worry only if the parent fish involved seems to be developing an appetite for its own caviar, a situation which can develop at times. Keep the parents well fed and this is less likely to happen.

If the parents do begin eating the eggs obviously faster than they are going bad, the most logical thing to do next is either to remove the parents or remove the eggs. Since you have gone this far in an effort to let nature take its course, you may wish instead to try and "divert" them either with food or even by introducing another fish, perhaps another angelfish of a bit smaller size. This can have the effect of having the pair unite their efforts against the intruder in defense of their progeny and make them forget about eating the eggs.

When hatching occurs, the fry become a quivering mass of almost jelly-like appearance. They remain adhered to the surface, although again an occasional one will fall to be swooped down upon, perhaps chewed around a bit, and replaced. At a temperature of 80 to 82°F., which is a good breeding temperature for angelfish although they will breed at somewhat higher and lower temperatures, the babies will be free-swimming in about five days after hatching. During this period, the babies are living on the nourishment provided by the yolk sac, which looks at first after hatching like a very large belly to which a tail and a little pair of eyes are attached. Over the period of time between hatching and free-swimming, the yolk sac is slowly absorbed, and when this absorption is completed, the now-slenderized youngster is no longer helpless and is able to swim about on his own.

During the time preceding free-swimming, parental care consists of alternate turns hovering over the babies, fanning them to provide adequate aeration and periodically picking them up in their mouths, "chewing" them around a bit in order to clean them, and spitting them back onto the slate or leaf. If other slates, leaves or suitable sites are available, the babies will be transferred to new locations perhaps several times. Sometimes during these moves one parent will stand guard while the other transfers youngsters; at other times both may participate in the move. The youngsters are again cleaned by mouth before being deposited.

Just barely visible in the plants above this pair of parent angels is a group of their hatched but not yet free-swimming fry. The parents are standing guard attentively and will periodically mouth the fry and then return them to their resting place. A closer view of the fry among the vegetation can be seen on page 87.

The transition to free-swimming occurs within an amazingly brief period of time, and often the aquarist will simply notice that the entire group has suddenly risen and become a school of remarkably competent swimmers. At this point they are hungry and in search of food.

Young black angels in a rearing tank. The babies are heavily fed for fast growth, and mystery snails are maintained in the tank to pick up leftovers that the baby angels might miss.

Free-swimming baby angelfish are larger than many other newborn egglayers such as zebra danios and three-spot gouramis, and they are perfectly capable of eating newly hatched brine shrimp as their first food. Brine shrimp, *Artemia salina*, are familiar to most aquarists. They are small saltwater crustaceans whose dormant eggs are sold in dry form to be placed in salt water and hatched at the time they are needed. The tiny shrimp which hatch from the dried eggs are just bitesize for many baby fishes, including angels. After hatching they are simply removed from the salt water in which they hatched and placed in the aquarium with the baby angels or whatever fish are to be fed; they will remain alive for several hours or until they are eaten. There is no better food for baby angelfish. It is clean and sterile, available when you need it and conducive to rapid growth. Complete instructions for hatching shrimp eggs and harvesting the baby shrimp are supplied with the eggs.

Baby angelfish, like other baby fish, should never be fed until they are free-swimming. At this point, however, they should be fed as soon as possible and in order to have groceries available at the proper time the first hatch of shrimp eggs should be put on a couple of days before the babies are to be free-swimming. Another hatch can be put on the next day, and on the following day the first hatch can be harvested and another started. By harvesting and re-starting the shrimp on alternate days in this manner, a fresh hatch is ready to come off each day.

Other living first foods such as microworms and sifted *Daphnia* can also be fed either instead of or in addition to newly hatched brine shrimp. Microworms are tiny worms which can be easily cultured by millions in refrigerator dishes or other receptacles which can be covered. The culture medium can consist of cooked oatmeal or pablum which has been prepared and mixed with brewer's yeast, and after introduction of a small portion of an old microworm culture, within a few days the entire surface is covered with the tiny creatures, and many can be seen just above the surface of the culture all around the sides of the containers. By placing two blocks of wood in the middle of the culture, one of which is half immersed with the other resting on top, the worms can be harvested simply by removing the upper block when its sides are seen to be covered with worms and rinsing the block in the aquarium containing the fish to be fed. The reason for using the two blocks is to allow the worms to climb free of the culture so that the rather messy culture medium

A microworm culture.

Nauplii of the saltwater crustacean *Artemia salina*. These baby brine shrimp are alive, but baby brine shrimp also are available in frozen form.

won't get into the aquarium. Those which climb to the upper block can be considered "clean." In a couple of weeks or so the culture may become too sloppy and too odorous to continue using. Simply prepare a new mixture of yeast and oatmeal and "seed" the new culture with perhaps a spoonful of the old. Temperature greatly affects not only the rate of production but also how long the culture lasts before it begins to smell as if you have your own private brewery going.

Daphnia are small freshwater crustaceans which are often called "water fleas." Sifted *Daphnia* are the tiny newborn individuals and are so called because they can be sifted through a fine sieve which will retain the larger ones. Sifted *Daphnia* and other similar crustaceans which sometimes occur with them such as *Cyclops* are comparable in size and suitability as a first food to newly hatched brine shrimp, although brine shrimp are superior in nourishment and have the advantage of being always available by hatching, while *Daphnia* and similar live foods are seasonal and otherwise variable in availability.

Other foods can also be used in a pinch, and with success. Perhaps the best is frozen baby brine shrimp, which as far as nourishment is concerned is equivalent to living newly hatched shrimp. The major difference, especially during the first few days of feeding, is that the shrimp don't move like live ones and sink to the aquarium bottom in a short while. The movements of living shrimp are definitely attractive to the baby fish, and since they remain alive for several hours they provide a continuing source of first class food during this time. Frozen shrimp must be fed more carefully, since those which are not eaten begin to deteriorate immediately. Judgment must be used so that more shrimp is not fed than can be eaten. While babies can be raised exclusively on frozen baby brine shrimp, this food will be more eagerly accepted if live shrimp are fed for the first few days at least.

There are other foods for baby fishes which can be used successfully with angels, but prepared foods, although they have been vastly improved in the last few years and many innovations have been introduced including several "fry foods" which are good, are best to be used in a supplementary capacity at least until the youngsters are well on their way. When the babies begin to look like baby angelfish, with the dorsal and anal fins beginning to lengthen and the ventrals or feelers also beginning to grow long, small quantities of supplementary foods can be added to their diet in between feedings of live food even in cases where one has all the live shrimp needed. Use food of highest quality which is small enough and feed *sparingly*, because baby angels are not unlike our own children when it comes to trying a new dish; until they get used to it they may leave most of it on the plate. Brine shrimp should still be the basic food if at all possible, since it is unexcelled in its ability to produce growth and vigor.

The parent fish, although they will eat along with the youngsters when they are given brine shrimp or other foods, should be fed as usual. Most aquarists prefer to drop the food for the adults outside the immediate area in which the babies are schooling at a given time in order to avoid any young being accidentally consumed by a parent in its enthusiasm for the food. Ordinarily, however, they are quite good at discriminating between groceries and offspring . . . unless they no longer wish to discriminate.

At night when the lights go out, the babies are herded into a corner or other place selected by the parents and bedded down. Bedding down amounts to a period of relative inactivity in which the school is much more tightly compacted. Straying is not tolerated, and any youngster rambunctious enough to attempt to wander is immediately collected and spit back into its proper place with such authority that the entire group soon becomes very quiet. When daybreak comes or the light otherwise returns, activity picks up, the school resumes its more normal and less concentrated configuration and the parents again escort them about the aquarium.

When angelfish are raised in this reasonably natural way, casualties seem to occur from time to time in the early stages which somewhat reduce the numbers of the progeny. While this is more than amply compensated by the chance to observe the family group, by the time the babies have been swimming for a week or so you may have only a hundred or fewer even from a fairly large spawn. There is an excellent chance, however, that these youngsters are among the strongest and most robust and remain surviving partially because they possess that little extra spark of vigor and vitality which sets them apart.

Hatching Eggs Separately

By far the majority of domestic angelfish which reach the aquarium market have never seen, much less been raised by, their parents. Nature, in her infinite wisdom, compensates for production rates. The millions of eggs of the codfish eventually dwindle to only enough individuals to sustain the race, while the few but highly developed offspring of the tiny livebearer *Heterandria formosa* accomplish the same purpose of sustaining the species with a much different approach. Nature takes into account natural losses, and Man attempts to intervene and alleviate these losses for the sake of increased production. This is true not only in the case of aquarium fishes but also in the case of game fishes such as black bass, trout and channel catfish which are hatchery-raised and released by millions each year for improved fishing for America's sportsmen. By removing angelfish eggs from the parents, hatching and raising them in separate facilities, production is tremendously increased. Professional breeders, who naturally are concerned with production, would never think of letting the eggs remain with the parents.

Another consideration is that mutations, individuals which are different from the ordinary, are often the first to be destroyed by parents as well as predators, apparently simply because they are "different." They are also sometimes less vigorous and need more attention than normal fish. If the mutations which occasionally turn up are attractive ones such as those which led to the eventual establishment of black lace, black, veil, marble or other popular strains, being the first to produce them or even being among the early breeders of the new strain can lead to quite a financially rewarding situation. There is also the fact that increasing the number of individuals produced increases the odds of one day obtaining a new and worthwhile mutation.

Egg Removal

Nature has programmed angelfish with instinctive protection of their eggs and offspring. So strong is this instinct that they will, at breeding time, literally attempt to fly in the face of any impending threat, including Man. When you reach for the eggs of your breeders, chances are you will be attacked with all the fury they can muster. In spite of the obvious weight advantage enjoyed by the aquarist, more than one otherwise brave individual has been seen to retreat before the furious onslaught of parent angels as an attempt was made to rob them of their spawn. The unnerving part is that they often seem actually to think they are going to win, and fly at the hand of the intruder as if it is their intention to dismember it. The assault, however, is harmless, much more so than that of the first setting hen I remember reaching naively under in order to check how many eggs she had.

If spawning takes place in a planted community tank on a swordplant or *Sagittaria* leaf or the like, the leaf must be cut. A swordplant leaf can be cut at the stem, while sag or similar plants which exhibit more uniformity of size all the way to the base can either be cut a few inches below where the lowermost eggs are or can be "stripped" by inserting a finger between the leaf to be removed and the remaining leaves which form the remaining body of the plant and pushing down with the fingertip while pulling slightly away. The rather firm, succulent and crisp base of the leaf will separate from the plant just below the gravel in most cases if the plant is properly planted. The leaf can be weighted when it is removed to the hatching receptacle by either placing a rock on the stem or attaching a small piece of lead to it. Some aquarists use a stainless steel safety pin, inserting it through the stem and then closing it.

Some of the angelfish eggs have hatched, and the newly emerged babies are seen as tails with food supplies attached.

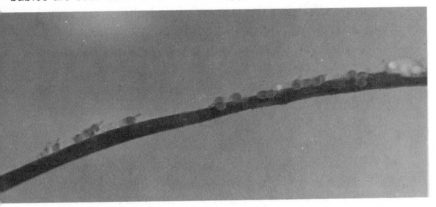

If a slate or tube of some sort is the chosen location for deposition of the eggs, it is simply removed and placed in the hatching container.

In either case, the container should have been prepared to receive the eggs before they are to be removed by providing proper water at the proper temperature. Water for hatching the eggs should be less than 100 ppm hardness and between 6.8 and 7.2 pH. If local water is too hard, distilled water can be added to dechlorinated tap water until the proper consistency is reached. If possible, use water which was distilled in glass instead of copper, although this is not always possible to determine.

Water can be used which has been softened by ion exchange either in a commercial household unit or with a softening pillow made for aquarium use. Softening water can sometimes produce chemicals which will raise the pH of the water, so this should be checked and corrected before use.

A wide-mouthed gallon jar such as pickles or mayonnaise are packed in for restaurants, etc., is a suitable hatching container, although a small aquarium will do as well. The leaf or slate should be placed in the jar or aquarium so that an air stone can be placed beneath it. Eggs should face upward so that the stream of air bubbles does not hit them directly. While methods and opinions vary, I prefer rather vigorous aeration, but not enough to dislodge the eggs from the surface to which they are stuck. Enough Methylene Blue should be added to the water to make it a deep blue, so blue in fact as to hardly leave the eggs visible.

During hatching, eggs which turn white due to in-fertility or fungus should be carefully removed. This may be done with a needle, eye dropper or a basting syringe. If the latter is used and an egg or two which are still good happen to be picked up, they may be gently squirted back onto the original spawning surface. This does no harm since the treatment is certainly no rougher than that of the parents when moving or cleaning their eggs or offspring. A few of the eggs may fall to the bottom of the jar, which does them no harm. They can either be picked up with the syringe and re-deposited or left until they hatch.

After hatching, the activity of the youngsters increases daily, and it is usually only a short while before at least some of the still-helpless little wrigglers have shaken themselves loose from their anchorage and fallen to the bottom.

Because of currents set up in the jar or other hatching container of your choice, the fallen youngsters will often wash to the same area and will stick together in a "ball" because of the adhesive substance which previously had them adhering to the leaf, slate or tube spawning location. They can either be re-deposited at the original site or left on the bottom, although aeration should be quite vigorous if the latter course is taken. The reason for this is that the mass of stuck-together individuals makes it a bit more difficult for adequate oxygen to reach all of them since some may be clustered at the center. The mucuslike, sticky substance which glues them together will be easily visible, as it absorbs much of the Methylene Blue, which is a dye, if you choose this as suggested as a fungus deterrent.

Sooner or later, replacing the babies is a lost cause and they end up on the bottom in a mass. If the spawn is large and the mass becomes thick, I have always preferred to break it up occasionally by blowing it apart with a stream of water from the basting syringe. Many breeders don't bother with this, depending on good aeration and the natural vigor of the young to get them through this period.

For those who want a "formula," here is one given to me years ago by one of the most successful breeders of angelfish I have ever known; he used it to raise many thousands of angelfish for retail and wholesale marketing. At the time, angels were still considered tricky, especially in his area, and the formula was considered "secret," although there is really not that much to it.

Water, which in this case was dechlorinated tap water and measured about 75–100 ppm hardness or about 5 DH and a pH of about 7.4 (a bit higher than usually recommended) was used which was at 80–82°F. and a 1-gallon pickle jar was the hatching container. To the gallon jar of water which was tilted and filled perhaps three-quarters full, three drops of 10% Methylene Blue was added. Aeration, and he considered this *most* important, was extremely vigorous. Each day after hatching, one-half the water was replaced with aged tap water at the same temperature. By the time the babies were swimming the water was only slightly blue. Live brine shrimp (newly hatched) were fed from free-swimming exclusively until the babies started to look like angels in form. The "extremely vigorous" aeration which he described was just short of turbulent, but he believed in the natural vitality of the youngsters and felt that they were not at all detrimentally affected by the heavy aeration. Aeration should be slowed after the babies have become free-swimming. Temperature control is very important from the time the eggs are deposited throughout the entire procedure. With 80°F. as a median temperature, this should not fluctuate more than plus or minus two degrees, which gives actually a 4-degree span. Greater fluctuation than this, especially at lower temperatures, can greatly weaken baby angelfish. With more delicate varieties like blacks, steady temperatures are imperative during the first days of their lives or they simply will not have the strength to become free-swimming.

A good way to control the temperature in the hatching jar is to keep it immersed in an aquarium containing an accurate thermostatically controlled heater. While there are plenty of inexpensive heaters and thermometers available that are quite serviceable for many aquarium situations, for breeding angels, or any other tropical for that matter, I suggest selecting a high quality, reliable and accurate heater and an accurate thermometer. Cutting corners with cheap merchandise is false economy more often than not, and certainly in this case it is.

One of the reasons for using a gallon jar for starting the young angels is that they have no trouble finding their food during their first days. Obviously, several hundred babies will soon outgrow the facilities. By having floated them in the aquarium which is to be their next quarters, there are few problems. Temperature is identical, and even if the water is a bit different in composition they can be acclimated by tipping a little of their water out at a time and tipping a little of the water from the aquarium in. Unless the water is extremely hard, the babies can be released in a few days before they begin to feel crowded.

A bare aquarium with a sponge-type filter such as those mentioned before is a good choice. Fifteen gallons is a good size at this point, allowing plenty of room to grow without having too large an area for the food to become scattered over. By the time they begin to outgrow this and require larger housing facilities, those with best potential for size, color or other characteristics will have started to show up and you may wish to give them separate facilities and special treatment when the move is made. A smaller size aquarium such as a 5-gallon can also be used if circumstances call for it, but use of a small tank will necessitate moving the babies earlier.

With large quarters and live food several times a day, angels can be salable in six to eight weeks, although they will still be rather small. Frequent partial water changes help stimulate their growth, and a 30- to 50-gallon aquarium will usually house an average-sized spawn until marketing size. Beyond the body size of a dime, growth may be retarded by trying to keep too many in the same aquarium. While nickel-size angels generally bring a better price than dime-size, it is best to sell some off rather than overcrowd them.

If you plan to continue breeding angelfish, be sure to hold back the best youngsters for your future breeding stock.

DISEASES OF ANGELFISH

Angelfish are apparently less subject to common diseases than most other fishes, and the diseases that they do come up with occasionally are few in number. Even ich, or ichthyophthiriasis, the most common of fish diseases found in the aquarium, seldom affects grown scalares in comparison to other fishes, although young fish up to perhaps half grown sometimes are infected. Instances of "pop-eye" and "hunger strike," which at one time seemed to affect scalares more than other diseases, have almost become past history. This is probably because the practice of regularly collecting live foods from questionable sources has become less prevalent. It is now possible to take angels and other carnivorous fishes from the beginning of life to its end a number of years later supplying them with perfectly good nutrition which is "clean," on such as frozen brine shrimp, live brine shrimp, beef heart, flake foods, freeze-dried foods and a host of other excellent choices. This probably has done more than anything to eliminate some of the weird diseases which sometimes seemed to come from nowhere a few years back. Not that live food should not be collected and used if one chooses, since this is one of the great pleasures of fishkeeping; it is just that extremely unclean sources be avoided and that if possible the food should be cleaned up a bit and sorted before using. A couple of changes of water can usually accomplish this.

"Ich" or Ichthyophthiriasis

Ichthyophthiriasis, better known in the aquarium hobby as "ich," is the most common disease of aquarium fishes.

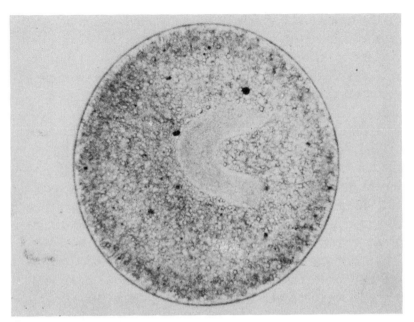

The ich parasite

Not only is it most commonly encountered, it is also the most commonly prescribed for in aquarium literature, and there has been historically a greater proliferation of "ich cures" on the market than for any other fish malady.

Also known as "white spot disease" or simply "white spot" because of the appearance of the encysted adult parasite on infected fish, ich is caused by the protozoan parasite *Ichthyophthirius multifiliis*. It is a parasite of warm-water and temperate water fishes, and although angelfish are less susceptible than many other tropicals, they occasionally become victims of the disease, especially when kept with others which become infected and need to be treated.

Ich goes through three definite stages: (1) the adult parasite which lives in the skin of the host fish, feeding on the tissue and body fluids of the fish and which appears as the white spot mentioned previously; (2) the mature parasite which leaves the host and falls to the bottom where it divides into (3) as many as 2000 free-swimming youngsters which all seek a host fish to which they may attach. Most treatments are effective only in the free-swimming stage.

The life cycle of the ich parasite is quite variable in the length of time it takes to complete, and this is affected by the temperature. Higher temperatures cause the cycle and all its stages to be completed faster, and for this reason temperatures of 80 degrees or slightly higher are often used as part of the treatment. This gives the free-swimming parasites less time to find a host before they die and also exposes them more quickly to the medication while in this susceptible stage.

There are a number of effective ich remedies on the market which can be obtained from your fish dealer.

Pop-Eye or Exophthalmia

Pop-eye or exophthalmia (exophthalmus) has been one of the more often encountered diseases of angelfish or scalares, although it could not be considered common. Actually, exophthalmia is a symptom, not a disease, and it can have a number of causes. Some of these are incurable, although others can be cured upon occasion.

Bulging or protruding eyes, as the name "pop-eye" implies, are symptomatic of this malady. The condition can be caused in some instances by not making partial water changes frequently enough, which results in a build-up of dissolved waste products in the water. Pop-eye can also be caused by *Ichthyosporidium*, which is a parasitic fungus. Other symptoms of this disease, which is also known as *Ichthyophonus*, are usually present also when it is the cause of pop-eye. These symptoms are bloody spots, body sores, tumors which have erupted, staggering, black spots, loss of fins, emaciation or scale protrusion. The disease is usually introduced with other fish and is considered incurable, although some success has been noted with 1% phenoxetol at about 50cc per gal. of water. Bacterial infections can also cause pop-eye. Treatment for bacterial diseases can be given by administration of 50 mg. per gal. of Tetracycline or Terramycin added to aquarium water every other day, or mixing with food at the rate of 200 mg. antibiotic to 4 oz. of food. Feeding should continue 10 days. Fish tuberculosis can also be responsible for pop-eye. Since fish tuberculosis is a bacterial disease caused by such as *Mycobacterium*, the same antibiotics can be used in the same manner for treatment if this is the suspected cause.

An angelfish exhibiting an ulcerated eye.

An important point to remember is that fishes of all kinds, especially angels, are much less subject to bacterial infections in a clean, well-filtered aquarium. Fishes which have been subjected to stress of one kind or another seem more susceptible. With good care and clean conditions, including regular partial water changes and removal of collected sediment, pop-eye is not likely to occur.

There is also a form of pop-eye which is otherwise known as "worm cataract disease" in which the eyes bulge and the cornea becomes cloudy because of the invasion of parasitic trematodes, or flukes, which are types of flatworms. These must live through a stage in which snails play the part of an intermediary host, and if they do not find a fish host within a very short period after leaving the snail, probably as little as an hour, they will die. Once a fish is infected there is no effective cure.

Although this form of pop-eye has been observed in angelfish, the parasite has invariably been introduced with snails, so wild snails should be avoided. Aquarium snails present no problem, since they are not exposed to water birds which serve as another intermediary host and from which the snails must become infected.

Hunger Strike

Loss of appetite and eventual complete refusal to eat was at one time one of the major problems with angelfish. This malady, which was generally known as "hunger strike," was attributed to various causes, among which were boredom with diet, chill, fright, improper pH and internal parasites.

While such things may have played their part, the basic problem seems to have been poor aquarium hygiene of one kind or another. Most authorities were at one time recommending "old water," which meant water in which fish and plants had been kept for a long time. Rainwater, which was obviously low in mineral content, was recom-

Angelfish usually are not very picky feeders and will accept most normal aquarium fare, but they sometimes go on a hunger strike and refuse to accept anything offered. But a change of water and the chance to eat something especially tempting (live baby livebearers are ideal for tempting adult angels) generally get them back on feed.

No system of aquarium filtration now in use can completely eliminate the dissolved pollutant factors in the aquarium, nor can plants absorb all of the fishes' waste products, so periodic water changes are necessary.

mended for replacement of evaporated water, and often an aquarium was kept without even partial change until it had turned to a deep yellow or almost gold color. Actively growing plants were supposed to utilize the waste of the fishes, in effect purifying the water and keeping it in what supposedly was close to original condition but with the added benefit of having been properly aged in the presence of fishes.

We now realize that even under ideal conditions, plants cannot absorb all the waste produced by well-fed fishes, and even should the obvious solid waste be removed by filtration or syphoning, there must be a buildup of dissolved waste products and urine in the water. This can eventually become so thick that it becomes detrimental to both fish and plants.

Frequent partial water changes eliminate this buildup and also a number of associated problems. Contrary to the beliefs of a few years ago, regular removal of aquarium water and replacement with fresh water stimulates the growth of plants as well as the appetites of fishes. This is particularly true with discus and angels, and in both cases they exhibit their best growth rates, heartiest appetites and highest degree of activity and enthusiasm when the practice of regular water changes is implemented.

If 25% of the water in an angelfish aquarium is changed weekly or even bi-weekly, hunger strike will seldom be a problem. A variety of foods should be offered and the temperature should preferably be kept at about 75 degrees or more. Filters should be changed regularly and questionable live food avoided.

CONCLUSION

Among the multitudinous array of fishes of every size, shape, habit, form and color imaginable which can be kept by the aquarist of today, only a handful are so completely satisfying in themselves as to be kept by many aquarists exclusive of other fishes. The angel, king of the aquarium, is unique for its qualities which make it deserving of this title. It is large, beautiful and spectacular, and yet for its size it is gentle. It is priced within the reach of any aquarist, but carefully developed and cultivated it can become a priceless show fish. It can grace the aquarium community, or fully compliment the largest show aquarium only with its own kind. Its breeding can provide a source of income or a source of challenge, and can be equally fascinating to those who enjoy procreation of creatures from its simplest point of view or to the geneticist whose interests stem further.

The angelfish is Nature at its finest, domestication near its peak.

Long live the King.